D1710610

Identity Theft

Jim Whiting

INCONTROVERSY

ReferencePoint Press®

San Diego, CA

© 2013 ReferencePoint Press, Inc.
Printed in the United States

For more information, contact:
ReferencePoint Press, Inc.
PO Box 27779
San Diego, CA 92198
www.ReferencePointPress.com

LIBRARY OF CONGRESS CATALOGING-IN-PUBLICATION DATA

Whiting, Jim, 1943–
    Identity theft / by Jim Whiting.
        p. cm. -- (In controversy)
    Includes bibliographical references and index.
    ISBN-13: 978-1-60152-454-6 (hbk.)
    ISBN-10: 1-60152-454-4 (hbk.)
    1. Identity theft--United States--Juvenile literature. I. Title.
    HV6679.W45   2013
    364.16'330973--dc23
                                                                          2012020139

Contents

Foreword

I n 2008, as the US economy and economies worldwide were falling into the worst recession since the Great Depression, most Americans had difficulty comprehending the complexity, magnitude, and scope of what was happening. As is often the case with a complex, controversial issue such as this historic global economic recession, looking at the problem as a whole can be overwhelming and often does not lead to understanding. One way to better comprehend such a large issue or event is to break it into smaller parts. The intricacies of global economic recession may be difficult to understand, but one can gain insight by instead beginning with an individual contributing factor, such as the real estate market. When examined through a narrower lens, complex issues become clearer and easier to evaluate.

This is the idea behind ReferencePoint Press's *In Controversy* series. The series examines the complex, controversial issues of the day by breaking them into smaller pieces. Rather than looking at the stem cell research debate as a whole, a title would examine an important aspect of the debate such as *Is Stem Cell Research Necessary?* or *Is Embryonic Stem Cell Research Ethical?* By studying the central issues of the debate individually, researchers gain a more solid and focused understanding of the topic as a whole.

Each book in the series provides a clear, insightful discussion of the issues, integrating facts and a variety of contrasting opinions for a solid, balanced perspective. Personal accounts and direct quotes from academic and professional experts, advocacy groups, politicians, and others enhance the narrative. Sidebars add depth to the discussion by expanding on important ideas and events. For quick reference, a list of key facts concludes every chapter. Source notes, an annotated organizations list, bibliography, and index provide student researchers with additional tools for papers and class discussion.

The *In Controversy* series also challenges students to think critically about issues, to improve their problem-solving skills, and to sharpen their ability to form educated opinions. As President Barack Obama stated in a March 2009 speech, success in the twenty-first century will not be measurable merely by students' ability to "fill in a bubble on a test but whether they possess 21st century skills like problem-solving and critical thinking and entrepreneurship and creativity." Those who possess these skills will have a strong foundation for whatever lies ahead.

No one can know for certain what sort of world awaits today's students. What we can assume, however, is that those who are inquisitive about a wide range of issues; open-minded to divergent views; aware of bias and opinion; and able to reason, reflect, and reconsider will be best prepared for the future. As the international development organization Oxfam notes, "Today's young people will grow up to be the citizens of the future: but what that future holds for them is uncertain. We can be quite confident, however, that they will be faced with decisions about a wide range of issues on which people have differing, contradictory views. If they are to develop as global citizens all young people should have the opportunity to engage with these controversial issues."

In Controversy helps today's students better prepare for tomorrow. An understanding of the complex issues that drive our world and the ability to think critically about them are essential components of contributing, competing, and succeeding in the twenty-first century.

From Riches to Rags

For years David Crouse enjoyed the convenience of being able to shop online for merchandise. He was a big fan of e-Bay and often downloaded music from iMesh. He paid for his purchases using an ATM card.

Crouse, who is in his late fifties, was aware of the potential dangers of Internet shopping. He thought that he was protecting himself from those hazards. He bought antivirus software and routinely updated it. He never wrote down his banking password. He shredded any documents that might contain sensitive information.

In spite of these precautions, early in February 2009 the Maryland resident noticed that a few strange charges were showing up on his monthly bank statement. They were not very large: thirty dollars here, seventeen dollars there, and he could easily cover them. He had a job as a government contractor that paid him well over $100,000 a year.

A Dramatic Change

Six months later, however, things changed dramatically. Crouse had recently lost his job, so his monthly income from unemployment insurance was just a fraction of what it had been before. At about the same time, there was an explosive growth in the bogus charges that were being posted to his account. "All of a sudden it really got bad," he says. "The charges hit big time—$600, $500, $100, $200—all adding up from $2,800 to $3,200 in one day."[1]

Much worse was to come. Crouse immediately contacted his bank. He filled out a form stating that the charges did not belong to him. The following day his bank posted yet another charge, this one for $4,000. In an effort to limit the damage, he visited the bank on a daily basis. That did not seem to help. Someone kept bleeding his account.

In desperation, Crouse changed banks. That did not help either. Within a day of making the change, charges appeared in both of his accounts. The sources of the charges ranged from Internet gambling sites to respected companies such as Dell. They included merchandise that was shipped to several states where he had never lived.

In the spring of 2010 a police detective in Ohio called Crouse. His credit information had been discovered in the trunk of a car that had been seized following the arrest of its driver.

A Huge Stack of Paper

By that fall, Crouse had accumulated a foot-high stack of paper that represented all the bogus purchases that had been charged to his accounts. This stack represented nearly a million dollars. In addition, he had paid nearly $100,000 out of his own pocket trying to fight whoever had made these charges. Both his savings and

Online shopping and bill paying are easy and convenient, which is why so many millions of people around the world have switched to the Internet for day-to-day business transactions. But, as Maryland resident David Crouse learned, it can also leave a person vulnerable to identity theft.

retirement funds had been depleted. His credit score had plummeted from a high figure to a level which virtually ensured he could not borrow money. And someone out there was still trying to open new accounts in his name.

The situation affected other areas of his life. He had two college-age sons, and he could not afford to pay for their continued schooling. One dropped out, and the other found a cheaper school.

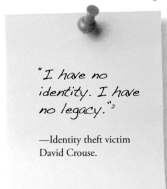

Even though he had an outstanding work history of many years, possessed a PhD degree in organizational psychology, and had worked for government agencies such as the Federal Bureau of Investigation (FBI) and Secret Service, Crouse struggled to find work. He had excellent interviews as he tried to find a new job, but no one would hire him. One recruiter finally told him that his low credit scores and mounting personal debt were keeping people from hiring him. Finally he found a job but with much lower pay.

A Fast-Growing Crime

He also had to forgo his longtime dream of celebrating his sixtieth birthday with a motorcycle trip across the United States. Crouse will be working—for as long as he can foresee. In the meantime, he lives very cheaply. He pays cash for his purchases, has regular payments taken from his checking account, and has little to look forward to as he struggles to get out of debt. "I have no identity. I have no legacy," he says. "My identity is public knowledge and even though it's ruined, they're still using it. It really ruined me. It ruined me financially and emotionally."[2] Not surprisingly, at one point Crouse was so depressed that he considered suicide.

Crouse was a victim of identity (ID) theft, which is one of the fastest-growing crimes in the United States—and the entire world. According to the Federal Trade Commission (FTC), "The term 'identity theft' means a fraud committed or attempted using the identifying information of another person without authority. The term 'identifying information' means any name or number that may be used, alone or in conjunction with any other information, to identify a specific person."[3]

Like Crouse, many people enjoy the convenience of being able to conduct more and more business online. But as he discovered, it can be risky. His story is becoming all too familiar to banks, credit card companies, and law enforcement personnel—and especially to the increasing number of individuals who have become victims of identity theft.

Facts

- According to *Time* magazine, 2.5 million dead people get their identities stolen every year.

- Seven percent of all US households had at least one member of the family at or over the age of twelve who had been a victim of some sort of identity theft in 2010, according to the US Justice Department.

CHAPTER ONE

What Are the Roots of the Identity Theft Problem?

I dentity theft has a long history. In the past, someone might murder another person and then assume that person's identity. Identity theft became less deadly and more common during the twentieth century, when new technologies arose and people began living in greater concentrations in urban areas. One common fraud was calling people on the telephone and telling them that they had won a prize. To claim it, they were told, they had to provide some personal information. Another was called "ghosting," in which identity thieves scoured obituary columns for names of the recently deceased or went to cemeteries to get names from freshly dug graves. Other methods included stealing mail and sifting through trash. They might also obtain personal information by purse snatching or picking people's pockets for their wallets.

Universal Identifiers

But it was the invention and proliferation of the Internet at the end of the twentieth century that led to the current explosive growth of ID theft. The Internet provides a number of relatively easy methods for thieves to steal identities from unsuspecting people, often without the victim even being aware of the theft. In many cases, the object of contemporary identity theft is to gain access to a person's Social Security number (SSN). That number provides the key that unlocks many doors that result in identity theft.

The Social Security System began in 1935 as a way of providing a small but dependable income for people when they reached retirement age. The original—and at that time only—purpose of having the nine-digit numbers was to keep track of participants' earnings during the years that they worked and then determine their eligibility for benefits when they retired. There was no intention of using it as a means of universal identification.

That situation has changed. As acting inspector general of the Social Security Administration (SSA) Patrick O'Carroll told a committee of the House of Representatives, "The SSN is a national identifier. In past years, many would challenge that statement. Today, we live in a changed world, and the SSN's role as a national identifier is a recognized fact. Unfortunately, with that knowledge, we must also accept that because the SSN is so heavily relied upon as an identifier, it is a valuable commodity for lawbreakers."[4]

The first big change in usage of SSNs came in 1961 when the Internal Revenue Service (IRS) began using them to track taxpayers. In turn, banks and other financial institutions needed the numbers to make sure they correctly reported interest and other forms of income. In the late 1960s the armed forces stopped using serial numbers for its members and replaced them with SSNs.
Since credit card companies were often closely connected with banks, it made sense to add them to customers' records as a means of keeping track through multiple address and/or name changes. This proved especially helpful with common names such as John Smith or Jane Smith. And the numbers had many other uses.

Even with this proliferation, access to SSNs remained somewhat limited until the invention and widespread usage of the Internet, starting in the early 1990s. While the Internet has revolutionized personal and corporate communications, it has also dramatically increased the opportunities for tech-savvy criminals to scam its users.

"We must . . . accept that because the SSN is so heavily relied upon as an identifier, it is a valuable commodity for lawbreakers."[4]

— Acting inspector general of the Social Security Administration Patrick O'Carroll.

Phishing

One of the main scams involves "phishing." The word is a variant spelling of "fishing." Scammers "fish" for gullible victims by dangling "bait" in front of them in an effort to "hook" them and

A 1936 poster urges Americans to obtain a Social Security number, which will be used later in life to receive monthly retirement benefits. No one imagined at the time that these numbers would become important national identifiers—and a lucrative information source for thieves.

thereby gain access to valuable information. The substitution of "ph" for "f" probably came from "phone phreaking," which originated in the 1970s and refers to cracking into telephone networks to make free long distance calls.

Phishing is basically pretending to be another computer, website, or link. It involves creating a website that appears to be legitimate and directing the user to it. The user clicks on the link, enters the requested data, and it is captured and sent to the phisher, who then has access to the victim's credit card or bank account information and can begin using it to make purchases.

Nearly everyone with an e-mail account receives phishing attempts on an almost daily basis. These might include:

- someone from a foreign country seeking to "purchase" products from the recipient and will ask for banking information to "deposit" the purchase funds;
- announcements from "foreign lotteries" that the recipient has been selected through a random computer process to win prizes often exceeding a million dollars;
- a lawyer or account manager in a foreign country, purporting to represent a person who has recently died and whose estate (valued at millions of dollars) is tied up by legal issues in that country, asking the e-mail recipient to help because of different laws in the United States;
- "Christian widows" (most commonly from small African nations) seeking help in releasing funds "for charitable purposes" from their dead husbands' estates, and offering a substantial portion of the funds to whoever helps them out;
- overseas companies such as hotels offering lucrative job openings that also include paid airfare, medical care, and accommodations;
- warnings from online publications, notifying subscribers that the credit card they use has been declined and asking them to update their card information.

The majority of such scams wind up in spam folders, sometimes accompanied by red banners noting that similar messages have been used to steal personal information and cautioning against clicking links or providing any personal information. Many can also be detected by the crude English that appears in the message, usually filled with typographical errors, improper punctuation, odd spelling and phrasing, and unconventional use of capital letters.

Bypassing Spam Filters

However, scammers may succeed in bypassing spam filters. Sometimes the subject line on a message in a person's inbox purports to come from a recognized bank and says something like "Temporary limit access to your account." Even though recipients may not recognize the bank nor believe that they have an account with it, some open the message anyway. According to the message, the account has been suspended for reasons such as "unauthorized login attempt" or "billing failure," and adds that the bank requires the recipient to update his or her account information by clicking on a link. Failure to do so, the message concludes, means that the account will be suspended and removed from the bank's database.

In recent years, phishers have become increasingly sophisticated. For example, Internet security expert Ondrej Krehel received a communication that appeared to be from Bank of America. It included a genuine Bank of America logo, and clicking on it took the user to the bank's authentic site. The color scheme was a perfect match to the real thing. Even drag-down boxes and places to type text were the same. "It's very sophisticated," Krehel says. "Hackers are creating these pages to look exactly like professionally crafted bank pages. So it does have the look and feel and touch of your bank's website. The text of the email is very well crafted. It looks like something Bank of America would actually send you."[5]

Spearphishing

A variation on phishing is known as spearphishing. Rather than setting a wide net to include as many people as possible as traditional phishing does, spearphishing zeroes in on individuals. In one form, the scammer pretends to be an individual who is trusted by the potential victim. For example, the scammer may know that an individual does business with a certain bank and sends the individual a "personal notice" that purports to come from that bank.

A Really, Really Big Whale

One unlikely victim of identity theft was Microsoft co-founder Paul Allen, who has a net worth of more than $14 billion. He owns the Seattle Seahawks and Portland Trail Blazers, plus a 400-foot yacht (122m) with a crew of sixty. Getting information about Allen and other prominent individuals is not terribly difficult. "On one hand, you can say that there's lots we can find out about the Paul Allens of the world," said Dennis Adsit, vice president of a company that develops security technology. "On the other hand, a guy like Paul Allen can hire and pay someone to scrub his information on the Internet, to make him more bulletproof."

Allen was not bulletproof enough for Brandon Price, identified by the FBI as an army deserter. Federal investigators say that Price called Allen's bank to change Allen's address to his own in Pittsburgh. Price called again three days later to say he had lost his debit card and needed a new one. When the replacement card arrived, Price used it to pay off a military loan of $658, then went shopping—at a dollar store and a video game store. While it is unclear how Price compromised Allen's account, the bank detected the fraud once he began accessing it. Authorities arrested him before he could complete a $15,000 Western Union transaction.

Quoted in Joann Loviglio and Randy Pennell, "If Microsoft Co-founder's ID Isn't Safe, Is Yours?," Associated Press, March 27, 2012. http://news.yahoo.com.

In another, the scammer might e-mail the victim at his or her place of work. While most organizations try to keep their employees' e-mail addresses confidential, it is not hard to access them. Many businesses allow callers to access employee names through an automated system based on pressing keys on a telephone. It only takes a few minutes to gain everyone's name.

Since many companies use one of several variations for e-mails, the scammer takes one of the names and tries possible combinations. Since most systems reject e-mails without valid addresses within a few moments, with a little patience the scammer can soon find the right combination. Once that information has been obtained, determined scammers can even send fraudulent e-mails that appear to come from someone within the company.

Whaling

A form of spearphishing known as whaling targets top executives at a company. Unlike traditional phishing, which sends the same impersonal message to large numbers of people, whalers carefully craft messages to specific personnel. According to InfoWorld, whaling is "aimed at senior executives or others in an organization who have access to lots of valuable or competitive information. While phishers generally go after consumers for bank account data, passwords, credit card numbers, and the like for financial gain, whalers most often target people who have inside information or can provide ongoing access to systems. Thus, the cost of being harpooned can be huge."[6]

Whalers take advantage of the fact that these busy executives may not take the time to thoroughly check out their communications. One executive received a note from the Better Business Bureau with the headline "customer complaint," then opened a link with details of the complaint. Another, a man with five children, received an e-mail offering a low-cost health care plan for large families. Clicking on the link allowed the whaler to gain access to the executive's computer, not only gaining insight into company operations but also letting him impersonate the executive.

A third attack in 2008 was a slight variation from usual whaling practice. It targeted thousands of top executives who received what appeared to be genuine subpoenas from the US Federal District Court in San Diego, which began:

Issued to: (Individual's name and title inserted here)

SUBPOENA IN A CIVIL CASE Case number: 94-621-PGM United States District Court

YOU ARE HEREBY COMMANDED to appear and testify before the Grand Jury of the United States District Court at the place, date, and time specified below.

Please download the entire document on this matter (follow this link) and print it for your record.[7]

The "subpoena" threatened contempt of court citations for failure to appear. A link provided the full text of the subpoena.

It proved surprisingly effective. Most antivirus programs could not detect it, and experts believe that at least two thousand executives became victims. Another who nearly did was Steve Kirsch,

Poor Grammar Provides Hint of a Scam

Members of vocational and social groups that a Washington state woman belonged to—and to which she was a frequent contributor—received an urgent appeal in March 2012. She said that during a visit to Aberdeen, Scotland, her bag with passport and credit card had been stolen. For unspecified reasons, she needed to return home as soon as possible. She explained that the American embassy would allow her to fly without a passport but that she needed money to pay for the ticket, and her credit card company could not act quickly enough. She urged everyone to help out and provided a link with contact information.

Many group members who knew the woman well suspected a scam. She is a professional editor. The posting was filled with errors of punctuation, grammar, and capitalization she would never make, even allowing for the supposed haste with which it was written. Not surprisingly, group message boards were flooded the following day with posts from people assuring everyone that it was a scam. Soon the real woman responded, apologizing profusely for what had happened.

CEO of a California antispam company. "I think that it was well done in terms of something people would feel compelled to respond to," he says. "It had my name, phone number, company and correct e-mail address on it and looked pretty legitimate. Even the U.R.L. to find out more looked legitimate at first glance."[8] Only when he forwarded it to his lawyer did the scam become apparent. Those who clicked on the link downloaded malware onto the executives' computers.

A blend of "malicious" and "software," malware involves the installation of harmful programs onto the victim's computer. David Crouse, for example, was a victim of keystroke malware. His computer got infected and picked up all his personal information by tracking every key he struck. That provided everything that the thief needed to get into his account: user name, password, challenge question(s), account numbers. Because the malware was still there when Crouse changed banks, it simply meant that he would be hit again.

In the case of the "subpoenaed" executives, the information was even more valuable. It involved crucial details of the operation of their companies. Once scammers had this information, they could sell it to competitors.

Vishing

A close relative to phishing is vishing. The primary difference is that instead of a bogus Internet link, vishers employ e-mail, instant messaging, or phone messages to say that an account has been suspended, deactivated, or terminated. To reactivate, the targets are asked to dial a phone number, which is provided in an e-mail or by a recording using Voice over Internet Protocol (VoIP) technology. This technology routes voice conversations over the Internet, and the "v" in "voice" accounts for the name of this method of deception.

During the call—which often imitates caller ID and seems to show the phone number of a genuine financial institution—the targets are asked to provide their credit card number and other information. The danger, according to Dawn Hicks of the Federal Reserve Bank of Boston, is that "while consumers have learned to be suspicious of phishing scams that involve solicitations for personal financial information directly over the internet, they are still easily persuaded to divulge that information when called directly or when an email instructs them to call a specific number."[9]

In a variation of vishing, victims receive a message about a supposed issue with their account via a voice message or e-mail, which also provides an 800 number to call to resolve the issue. That 800 number is connected to an automated attendant that permits victims to enter the requested information using their telephone touchtone keys. This information goes straight to a computer, which can automatically forward the stolen information anywhere. This system provides complete anonymity to the scammers and allows them to remain untraceable.

Thieves Profit from Social Networking Sites

Phishing and its offshoots are not the only ways in which identity thieves gather personal information. The dramatic increase in social media sites such as Facebook has created many opportunities for identity thieves. The FBI calls this type of ID theft social engineering. "With social engineering, what you can do is you can use other people and resources and not necessarily have to go in through the front door hacking through a computer," says FBI agent Alice Tsujihara, an ID theft specialist. "There is a lot of electronic information of our personal information stored over the Internet. . . . The more believable you are when stealing that person's identity, the more successful you're going to be."[10]

Diane Solomon of Santa Clarita, just north of Los Angeles, experienced this firsthand in 2010. Solomon was competing in a fun run in Los Angeles when she received a message from a neighbor. The neighbor said that she was, at that moment, talking to Solomon on Facebook. When Solomon told the neighbor that she did not have a Facebook account, she says the neighbor responded: "Well, you do this morning and I am talking to you. There's even a picture of you in the bowling ball costume from the Halloween party last year, and you're asking me for money."[11]

Earlier that day, Solomon had received a text message on her

"The more believable you are when stealing that person's identity, the more successful you're going to be."[10]

— FBI agent Alice Tsujihara.

Keeping up with friends and family and making new friends is the main appeal of online social networking, but users need to be wary of how much information and what type of information they share on their personal pages, especially if they do not use strong privacy settings.

cell phone. According to the text, her e-mail address had been changed. Someone had broken into Solomon's Yahoo account and used the Halloween photo to create a new—and entirely bogus—Facebook account. Posing as Solomon, the hacker sent a message to everyone in her Yahoo address book titled "My Plight." It was an example of the "stranded traveler" scam. This scam is becoming increasingly common, especially among Facebook users with large numbers of friends. "Basically it said I was traveling in London with my family and we were held up at gunpoint. Everything was taken but we still had our passports. We couldn't clear the hotel bill, we couldn't get home, and I needed some money,"[12] Solomon explains.

Solomon acted quickly, shutting down both the Facebook and Yahoo accounts. Even though she was entirely blameless, she still felt bad for exposing her friends—many of whom bought into the scam and were ready to send money—to possible repercussions had they done so.

Facebook and other social media sites have also given the so-called whalers a bounty of information for their exploits. "As more private information becomes public, through social media sites and otherwise, targeting specific individuals within companies has become easier for hackers and thus a preferred method of attack," says Kim Peretti, a security expert at the PricewaterhouseCoopers consulting firm. "This proliferation of information on individuals—where they work, with whom they interact socially and professionally, what conferences they attend, when and where they vacation—has enabled hackers to determine not only which individuals at companies may hold the keys to the kingdom, but also to which messages these [people] are most likely [to] be duped into responding."[13]

Too Much Information

Social networking sites offer other key pieces of information to identity thieves. People who include their birthdate and birthplace on their personal page and do not have strong privacy settings may unwittingly provide identity thieves the information they need to come up with a Social Security number. Until very recently, the first three digits were keyed to the state in which the number was issued. The next two were based on the order in which the particular number was issued—thereby providing a clue as to the relative age of the person.

A recent study by two Carnegie Mellon researchers revealed that given this information, ID thieves had a one in eleven chance of successfully guessing a complete SSN. The odds were considerably higher in small states, where after one thousand attempts the researchers had an accuracy rate of six in ten with people born recently. As *InformationWeek* writer Thomas Claburn explains, "The accuracy with which SSNs can be predicted in 100 attempts varies, based on the availability of online data and on the subject's date and place of birth, from 0.08% to over 10% for some states. Such odds may not seem particularly dangerous, but an attacker could use a computer program to guess and guess again, over and over. With 1,000 attempts, a SSN becomes as easy to crack as a 3-digit PIN [personal identification number]."[14]

Identity thieves took advantage of human nature when they flooded Facebook users with invitations to view the dead body of Osama bin Laden shortly after his death was made public in May 2011. Those who clicked on the link unwittingly activated malware on their computers.

Taking Advantage of Human Nature

What ID thieves depend on most is human nature. People like to share information about themselves with others, especially when that information reveals something new, positive, or exciting in their lives. Many people post their travel plans, for instance, but do not realize that such postings can alert a thief to a vacant house—and the potential for mining the information found in a mailbox. Once they look up the address, thieves can maintain watch over their victims' mailboxes and swoop in as soon as the postal carrier has moved on. Even those who are discreet about their own travel plans can accidentally betray their friends. Writing "Have a great time in Hawaii next week" on a friend's wall could make a potential identity thief's eyes open wide.

Human nature also came into play with a scam that circulated shortly after the death of Osama bin Laden in May 2011. Within a few hours after President Barack Obama went on national television to announce Bin Laden's death, Facebook users were flooded with invitations to view the dead al Qaeda leader's body. Fascinated by the idea of seeing the body of the mysterious 9/11 mastermind, people clicked on the links. In a classic phishing scam, that click activated malware. Says Krehel: "Social media are used to spread malicious software quickly because users will forward sensational sites to all their friends before they actually review the whole page. When they do, it's too late. They realize they've been scammed and phished."[15]

The Bin Laden message spread so widely and quickly that the FBI issued an official warning less than forty-eight hours after his death:

> The FBI today warns computer users to exercise caution when they receive e-mails that purport to show photos or videos of Usama bin Laden's recent death. This content could be a virus that could damage your computer. This malicious software, or "malware," can embed itself in computers and spread to users' contact lists, thereby infecting the systems of associates, friends, and family members. These viruses are often programmed to steal your personally identifiable information.[16]

Identity theft is the dark side of the ease and convenience that the Internet and easy online communication have provided. E-mails are subjected to phishing attacks on virtually a daily basis. And social media users can unwittingly provide thieves with a virtual gold mine of personal information and opportunities for attacks.

"Social media are used to spread malicious software quickly because users will forward sensational sites to all their friends before they actually review the whole page."[15]

— Security expert Ondrej Krehel

Facts

- People who have been Facebook users for five years or longer are twice as likely to suffer identity fraud than newer users.

- Two of the most common phishing scams claim to come from eBay and PayPal.

- A variation of phishing, known as pharming, seeks to hijack websites to a new location and make the original site impossible to reach.

- In 1961 the Civil Service Commission adopted Social Security numbers as official federal employee identifiers.

- An identity thief who stole credit card applications from the US Postal Service was arrested when authorities sifted through his trash and found incriminating evidence.

How Big a Problem Is Identity Theft?

Identity theft is one of the fastest-growing crimes in the United States. The FTC estimates that up to 10 million people may be victims each year. And according to research firm Javelin Strategy and Research, the situation is getting worse. The firm estimated the number of cases in 2011 at 12 million, a 13 percent increase over its 2010 estimate. More conservative estimates range from 3.2 million to 9 million. As Reuters reporter Mitch Lipka notes, "The rise in the use of smartphones and social media by incautious consumers fueled the increase in identity fraud. . . . Javelin found 62 percent of smartphone users do not use password protection for their home screens; this allows anyone who finds or takes their phones to have access to the contents."[17]

Identity theft was the top complaint received by the FTC in 2011 for the twelfth year in a row. Of 1.8 million complaints, 279,156, or 15 percent, involved identity theft. Experts believe this number understates the incidence of identity theft. Many victims either report the crime elsewhere or do not report it at all.

Hard to Investigate

Regardless of the precise number of people affected, identity theft is clearly a major problem in this country—and around the world. And it is likely to remain that way. One reason is that for law enforcement, identity theft is harder to investigate than robbery, murder, and other crimes. When police investigate crimes such as these, they spend considerable time at the crime scene gathering evidence, including fingerprints and DNA samples, and talking to witnesses.

A Global Problem

Although identity theft appears to be more common in the United States than in other countries, it is a global problem. In Canada, for example, a woman was victimized by a scammer who had a costly prosthetic leg operation in her name. Another Canadian spent three days in jail on income tax evasion charges by someone who had stolen his identity. A third, who lost his wallet in the United States, was arrested at the border several years later on manslaughter charges resulting from the theft of his identity.

In Singapore, a survey found that a majority of respondents view identity theft as a greater threat than terrorism or epidemics. "The top two areas of concern for the past few surveys have been consistently identity theft and credit/debit card fraud," says Scott Whyman, an executive with the company that conducted the survey.

Although identification, banking, and credit card practices vary from country to country, identity thieves have managed to obtain the information they seek from individuals, corporations, and government agencies worldwide. As contributing author for IdentityTheftSecrets.com Lisa Carey notes, "No country has been able to eliminate identity theft, and while the methods for obtaining information change it does not stop identity thieves from finding ways to obtain personal and financial information."

Quoted in Victoria Ho, "Identity Theft Is Still Asia's Top Concern," ZDNet Asia News, December 11, 2007. www.zdnetasia.com.

Lisa Carey, "Identity Theft Is Not Just for Americans," Ezine Articles. http://ezinearticles.com.

Identity theft is different. Without a traditional crime scene, uncovering vital physical evidence is impossible. In most cases no one can tell when the crime occurred. Often weeks, months, or years elapse before people realize they have become victims. And since the actual crime scene is a computer, there are no witnesses to provide helpful information.

Another complicating factor is that investigating identity theft is time- and labor-intensive. In an era where law enforcement budgets are being slashed, police departments give priority to violent crimes. Often little or no money is left over for less serious felonies. According to some estimates, examination of a single computer hard drive for possible evidence can consume dozens of hours.

Jurisdictional issues can also create problems for investigators. In many cases, the victim lives in one state and the financial charge to the victim's account takes place in another state. For example, people from all over the country order books and other items from Amazon, which is headquartered in Seattle, Washington. If an Amazon purchase is involved, the crime scene would be Seattle. But Seattle police might not have time to assist a victim who lives in, say, Virginia.

Sergeant Ed Dadisho of the Los Angeles Police Department points out yet another obstacle to investigating identity theft:

> Another challenge law enforcement could face is the lack of cooperation from some of the private financial institutions, and their unwillingness to increase security measures. Although the victim of the identity theft is the person whose name and identification was used, the financial institutions will pay off the actual losses. Once that occurs, the victim becomes the financial institution and unless there are major financial losses the institutions generally will not wish to prosecute.[18]

Ola Olatilu of the technology consulting and security company Conintava explains this unwillingness. "Customers and investors alike lose confidence related to any negative news of a corporation, especially when it is perceived that the due diligence required to safeguard customer information was absent. An unfor-

Police forensics experts gather evidence at a crime scene in Washington. The absence of a physical crime scene greatly complicates efforts to investigate crimes involving identity theft.

giving and major event can cause a corporation to lose credibility and business to a competitor. . . . Such an occurrence can be devastating to a corporation, possibly to an extent where it may not entirely recover."[19]

Who Is at Risk?

Identity theft captured the imagination of Frank Abagnale in the mid-1960s. While still a teenager, Abagnale began assuming a number of different identities to cash millions of dollars of bogus checks. His exploits were chronicled in a book he wrote and in the 2002 movie *Catch Me If You Can*. After being caught by the FBI, Abagnale turned his hard-earned lessons to helping law enforcement. Today Abagnale is one of the most respected figures in the field of identity theft. His list of who is a potential target for identity theft is sobering: "Anyone who has a credit card or a bank account, or who pays a bill. Anyone who has a mortgage, a car loan, or a debit card. Anyone who has a drivers license, a Social Security number, or a job. Anyone who has phone service or health insurance. Anyone who goes on the Internet. . . . In other words, anyone who's alive is a potential victim."[20]

Children are a particular target for identity thieves. IRS regulations stipulate that children must have Social Security numbers to be claimed as dependents. Yet few parents bother to monitor their child's credit history—since they assume there is none. As a result, children's SSNs are golden for identity thieves because they can use them for years without fear of exposure. In addition, many of these numbers are in sites—such as pediatricians' offices and schools—where there is little or no monitoring. According to a Carnegie Mellon University study in 2009–2010 involving 42,232 children, 4,311—more than 10 percent—showed evidence of identity theft.

Years later, victims face the consequences. Now thirty-one, Stephanie McManis had her identity stolen when she was just twelve. She spends considerable time dealing with collection agencies, banks threatening to sue for back payments, hospitals demanding reimbursement for emergency room visits she never made, and similar situations. "It's frustrating because I'm constantly having to jump through hoops," McManis says. "I'm resigned to the fact that I will be dealing with this for the rest of my life."[21]

> "Anyone who's alive is a potential victim."[20]
>
> — Security expert Frank Abagnale.

The Grandfather Scam

At the other end of the age spectrum, the so-called Grandfather Scam targets senior citizens. It plays on their desire to help their grandchildren when they get in trouble. After identifying potential victims, scammers use Facebook and other Internet sites to find as much information as possible—such as schools, favorite vacation spots, friends, favorite foods—about grandsons and granddaughters. In a typical situation, the scammer phones the grandparents and after identifying himself as their grandson, explains that he is in trouble and needs money wired right away. The information the scammer has gleaned provides a veneer of authenticity. The conversation usually includes something along the lines of "And please don't tell mom and dad. I'd be in a lot of trouble if they find out."

The grandparents are all too willing to go along, both with the request to send money and to keep the parents out of the transaction. "We've interviewed a lot of the cons who have done this kind of thing," said Doug Shadel, an official with the American Association of Retired Persons. "They find different ways to get you to react. What's more emotional than someone calling and posing as your grandson and your granddaughter?"[22]

One grandfather's initial payment of $4,300 for a supposed traffic accident in which his grandson was allegedly at fault eventually ballooned to more than $80,000. The additional funds were supposedly for lawyers' fees, bail, and medical treatment for the victim who claimed to have suffered a broken leg and miscarriage as a result of the accident. The grandfather explained that "I felt so concerned about my grandson. I wanted to do the right thing to get him released and home as soon as possible."[23] In reality, the grandson had been home during the entire episode. Everything the caller had told the young man's grandfather was bogus. While law enforcement officials believed they had located the scammers, the victim had no hope of recovering his money as it had long since been spent.

Fake Jobs

People who are unemployed and desperate to find jobs are also at risk of identity theft. In a poor economy with high unemployment, many people are tempted to take any job that comes along. They are tempted by Internet ads promising good wages for what seems to be minimal work. Many times the work is advertised as something that can be done from home, though its actual nature is never made clear.

Often these ads turn out to be scams, so much so that the Better Business Bureau of New York labeled them as the top overall scam of 2011. Persons may be hired on the basis of a phone interview, and scammers commonly create fake company websites. After the prospective employee has been told that he or she has the job, the scammers request an SSN to run what they say is a credit check. Or the new hire might be asked to provide detailed banking information to set up a system of direct deposits. Of course, no money actually comes in because no job exists. Rather, this information is used to tap into the victims' accounts, further depleting their meager financial resources.

Financial Fraud

Identity theft takes a number of different forms. The most common and far-reaching is financial identity theft, in which one person uses the identity of another person to obtain credit, goods, and services. According to authors James Munton and Jelita McLeod:

> Credit card fraud is the most common form of reported identity theft, followed by phone or utilities fraud, employment fraud, and bank fraud. Identity thieves can set up new credit card, phone, and utility accounts using the names and personal information of their victims. . . . Stolen identities are utilized to obtain loans, file fraudulent tax returns, forge documents, apply for government benefits, rent property, and do just about anything that requires a name, address, and Social Security number.[24]

While experts disagree about the full scope of financial identity theft, most agree that the losses run into billions of dollars. It has become so pervasive that some companies simply regard it as part of the cost of doing business. As Laura Bruce of Bankrate.com explains, "How many companies have fallen prey to an identity thief with a fraudulent credit card and have opted against pursuing charges because it would cost more than the amount the fraudster got away with? . . . Too often companies wrote off the loss as a cost of doing business."[25]

For example, an identity thief named John Phillips victimized a Connecticut man. Phillips wrote a series of bad checks totaling $4,042 for renting property in Virginia belonging to Sandbridge Realty. The firm's general manager, Cathy Ruizgonbert, explains that, "We're a small company; we don't have the staff to chase after this. We won't hire a lawyer or go out

"Stolen identities are utilized to obtain loans, file fraudulent tax returns, forge documents, apply for government benefits, rent property, and do just about anything that requires a name, address, and Social Security number."[24]

— Authors James Munton and Jelita McLeod.

Anyone who has a Social Security card, car loan, mortgage, and debit and credit cards is an enticing target for identity thieves. Information gleaned from any of these sources can be sold or used by thieves to assume a false identity.

of state. Sometimes you just say, 'I'm glad they're gone,' and you move forward."[26]

And death does not end the possibility that someone can suffer financial identity theft. Beginning in 2005, Tracy Kirkland of California exploited a loophole in the system to access the SSA's death index listing. It listed SSNs to keep banks and credit card companies from opening new accounts using the names of the recently deceased. Kirkland gathered as much information as she could about these people, then began calling credit card companies. She posed as the deceased to see if they had existing open accounts. If so, she put in a change of address and began using these accounts to make illegal charges. Before her arrest in 2008, prosecutors believe, she opened at least one hundred fake accounts. The following year she was convicted, sentenced to thirty months in prison, and ordered to make restitution of more than $180,000.

Mistaken Arrests

Another form of identity theft is criminal identity theft. According to the Internet Theft Resource Center, it may account for as much as 30 percent of all ID thefts. While perpetrators may use the stolen identification for financial gain, usually the major motivation is to avoid prosecution for other crimes. The criminal assumes the victim's name, SSN, date of birth, and other relevant data and uses this false identity when dealing with law enforcement and the court. The imposter then skips out on bail. Now a warrant is issued for the arrest of the unfortunate—and unsuspecting—victim. In some cases, the imposter is convicted of a crime, which then goes on the record of the victim and can emerge in situations such as job interviews (unless and until the identity theft is revealed and cleared up).

Often these situations come to light when the unaware victim is pulled over for what initially appears to be a minor traffic infraction. While checking the license and registration, the police officer learns of an outstanding warrant against this individual and performs the required arrest procedures. At the police station the bewildered victim is accused of having committed a crime and failing to appear at a subsequent court hearing. Eventually, after a comparison of fingerprints and mugshots reveals that this individual's identity had been used by someone else, the victim is released.

The process does not always flow so easily, and the victim may spend time in jail. And worse is to come. This innocent person now has a criminal record, and it may take considerable time and money to clear up the situation. "This is the ultimate humiliation, the ultimate nightmare if you ask me," says Jim Doyle, president of Internet Crimes Inc. "And it falls on the victim to clear up the criminal record."[27]

Imposter Wreaks Havoc on Victim's Life

The case of Malcolm Byrd of Janesville, Wisconsin, illustrates the difficulties that criminal ID theft victims may encounter. A man arrested on drug charges identified himself as Malcolm Byrd. The real Malcolm Byrd read an article about the arrest, went to the local police to report the situation, and thought that was the end of the problem. It was just the beginning. Four months later, he was pulled over for speeding. Moments later, he was facedown on the pavement and handcuffed. Police records still showed he was wanted on drug charges. The situation was soon cleared up. But he was fired from his job not long afterward, denied unemployment benefits, and could not renew his driver's license—all because of the criminal record.

Friendly Fraud

The image that most people have of identity thieves is a of stranger, often thousands of miles away. But according to Javelin Strategy and Research, one in seven identity theft cases involves someone the victim knows—a relative, friend, coworker, roommate, teammate, and so on. "It's something that people have to be aware of," says Anne Wallace, president of the nonprofit Identity Theft Assistance Center. "It's a difficult thing to protect yourself against because you are not expecting it."

According to Javelin, financial losses in cases involving identity theft by a relative, friend, or acquaintance may be greater—sometimes more than twice as much—than when identity theft is committed by a stranger. The thieves are likely to go undetected for longer periods of time. And their knowledge of the victims' personal habits is greater.

One noteworthy example came when Malikah Shabazz—the daughter of famous black activist Malcolm X, who was assassinated in 1965—pleaded guilty to identity theft involving Khaula Bakr, the seventy-year-old widow of one of her father's former bodyguards. Shabazz took out credit cards in Bakr's name and made $55,000 worth of purchases.

"The defendant, who preyed upon the trusting nature of a once-close family friend, has admitted her guilt in committing a serious felony offense and will be ordered to make her victims financially whole," said Queens district attorney Richard Brown.

Quoted in Eileen Ambrose, "When Friends and Family Are Identity Thieves," *Baltimore Sun*, April 25, 2011. http://articles.baltimoresun.com.

Quoted in Sheryl Huggins Salomon, "Malcolm X Daughter Pleads Guilty to ID Theft," The Root, June 10, 2011. www.theroot.com.

The following year, the imposter was arrested again, in a neighboring county, and again identified himself as Byrd. The real Byrd traveled there and received a court document proving his innocence. It did not matter when he was pulled over two years later. Again the handcuffs came out. Again he was taken to the police station before the situation was resolved.

The worst was yet to come. His niece was pulled over while driving his car, and police asked her where he was. Soon afterward, three officers with warrants from three counties came to his home. They arrested him in front of his two young children and threatened to take them to child protective services. This time he spent two days in jail before being released. "I don't feel safe now," Byrd said. "When we drive I feel uncomfortable. It's affected our lives enormously."[28]

Medical Identity Theft

Identity theft can even cross into the area of medical records and health care. In medical identity theft, someone uses the victim's name to obtain health care. In addition, the imposter escapes paying the (often substantial) bills he or she has incurred, saddling victims with having to pay them—or at least having to prove that they should not have to pay for care they never received.

In a way, this is the most dangerous form of identity theft as it can be life threatening. The victim's health records become "polluted" by the imposter, which can result in denial of much-needed treatments or misdiagnoses. Security authority Mari Frank, herself an identity theft victim and today one of the nation's leading authorities on the subject, points out an example of this pollution. "One client of mine was not allowed to renew her driver's license because her medical record stated that she had epilepsy," she writes. "A fraudster with seizures had used her identity to get medical treatment and credit."[29]

A Salt Lake City, Utah, woman named Anndorie Sachs received a call from a local hospital late in 2008. Her newborn baby had just tested positive for illegal drugs. The following day, a representative of the state's Child and Family Services agency came to her house and threatened to remove her four children because she clearly was an unfit mother. However, Sachs did not have a newborn baby. She had not given birth for several years. A twenty-eight-year-old pregnant drug abuser had stolen Sachs's driver's license and went to the hospital to give birth. She left the child behind and fled, leaving behind a bill for $10,000 that the hospital insisted be paid by Sachs. When hospital officials kept insisting that the baby was Sachs's, she had to submit to DNA testing to prove that she was not the mother.

In 2011 California benefits clerk Mia Garza was sentenced to twelve years in jail for stealing personal information of nearly thirty thousand Kaiser Permanente employees. One victim, Sierra Morgan, received a $12,000 bill for liposuction performed on Garza from a health care credit account Morgan had opened to pay for braces for her teeth.

In 2007 a Florida woman named Linda Weaver received a hospital bill for amputation of her right foot. Since she had both feet, she went to the hospital and easily proved that the surgery had been performed on someone else. This person had used her Social Security number and insurance identification number to have the procedure. That was not the end of Weaver's problems, however. A year later, she went into the hospital for an operation. The nurse said that she noticed that Weaver had diabetes. Weaver did not. The fraudster's medical information had become intermixed with her own. "I now live in a fear that if something ever happened to me, I could get the wrong kind of medical treatment,"[30] Weaver says.

Weaver's fear is genuine. Under the terms of HIPAA (Health Insurance Portability and Accountability Act), the federal law that addresses medical privacy issues, patients are entitled to copies of their medical records. But in *U.S. News & World Report,* writer Michelle Andrews points out an exception. "If an imposter gets healthcare in your name, you may really be stuck," she says. "Healthcare providers may actually refuse to let you see your own record because once it's intermingled with someone else's, that person's privacy must be respected."[31]

According to a 2011 study, nearly 1.5 million Americans have been the target of medical identity theft. This number is likely to increase as the costs of health care continue to rise and people desperate for medical attention seek any recourse. Writer Pamela

Lewis Dolan of *American Medical News* says that Phil Blank, senior security analyst at Javelin Strategy and Research, "cited the slow economy and more people losing insurance as drivers behind increasing medical identity theft."[32]

Dolan notes a twist on this theme. "Larry Ponemon, president and founder of the Ponemon Institute, a privacy research center based in Traverse City, Michigan, said his research has found nearly half of medical ID thefts are considered 'Robin Hood crimes,'" she says. "That means willing or sympathetic 'victims' lend their identity to someone else so that person may get needed services."[33]

Consequences of Identity Theft

Whatever form identity theft takes, it has numerous consequences. One is the actual loss of money, which can be considerable. People often do not pay much attention to monthly credit card statements and simply pay the amount shown. Even when they become aware of a problem, they may believe that they have to pay for what has been purchased in their name. Another consequence is the amount of time—and additional money—it takes to stop further thefts and reclaim one's identity. According to estimates, the actual financial outlay to stop the process is at least $1,500, and in many cases considerably more. And it is not uncommon for people to spend hundreds of hours on the phone, on the computer, or in person trying to reverse the process and restore their good name and credit.

Damaged credit can be the worst outcome of identity theft. The thief has often made large purchases in the victim's name without paying for them, which lowers the victim's credit rating and has numerous negative repercussions. Obtaining a loan is more difficult, and the interest rates and terms are less favorable. Many prospective employers look at a person's credit situation and may refuse to hire that person on the basis of bad credit. Victims may also pay higher rates on various forms of insurance or be turned down altogether and be unable to get new credit cards.

Even though the victim is completely faultless, the situation may take years to clear up. "In January 2009, Narcizo Zavala Guillen filed a police report after he became a victim of identity theft," writes Jessica M. Pasko in theidchannel.com. "Three years later, Mr. Guillen is still fighting a court battle to repair his damaged credit report and get debt collectors off his back. Guillen's attorneys allege that inaccurate information has continued to be listed on his credit report, despite numerous requests that credit agencies CREDCO, Trans Union and Experian re-investigate and correct the mistakes."[34]

Emotional Damage

The consequences of identity theft often go beyond time and money. Victims forced to contend with identity theft issues on an ongoing basis may experience lasting emotional difficulties. Dadisho notes that "identity theft is an emotionally abusive crime, and its psychological effects on the victim may last for years. It is a repetitive crime, as victims receive continual notices by phone or mail from creditors. Therefore, victims suffer some of the same emotional damage as victims of repeated physical assault."[35]

> "Identity theft is an emotionally abusive crime, and its psychological effects on the victim may last for years."[35]
>
> — Los Angeles Police Department sergeant Ed Dadisho.

Jessica Van Vliet, assistant professor in counseling psychology at the University of Alberta in Canada and author of a recent study of the victims of identity theft, adds that victims may never attain a sense of closure. "It was very clear that most participants in the study no longer felt safe conducting everyday financial transactions that most of us take for granted," she says. "No matter how well they monitor their financial records for the rest of their lives, they may still feel vulnerable."[36]

Clearly, identity theft has pervaded almost every level of society. Literally everyone is at risk, from toddlers to the elderly. And the costs can barely be estimated, both in terms of money and of long-lasting psychic scars.

Facts

- A 2007 spot-check in Utah revealed that nine different people were using a nine-year-old's Social Security number to gain employment, according to Utah assistant attorney general Richard Hamp.

- People from the ages of twenty-five through thirty-four are most likely to be the victims of friendly fraud.

- In October 2011 police in New York City arrested a ring of 111 identity thieves, the largest takedown of its type in US history.

- According to a 2011 study, the average cost to resolve a case of medical identity theft was $20,663—up from $20,160 in 2010.

- Washington, DC, has the highest rate of identity theft complaints—150.4 per 100,000 population—followed by Nevada (106) and Colorado (95).

- Eight percent of identity theft complaints come from victims nineteen and younger.

CHAPTER THREE

How Serious a Threat Are Hackers?

Phishing and other attacks on individual sites normally involve accessing that individual's computer remotely and manually cracking passwords to gain access to personal data. But these attacks are not the only form of threats to personal identity. Some hackers launch direct attacks on government sites, financial institutions, and corporations where the potential damage is massive in scale.

Data breaches, as these attacks are called, involve anything that puts someone's name and sensitive information—Social Security number, driver's license number, financial information such as credit card numbers, medical records, and more—potentially at risk. Hundreds of these breaches occur every year and can potentially compromise millions of sensitive records. While not all breaches are caused by hackers, hacking has become the leading cause. Many experts believe that data breaches are increasing in number and scope. "Skilled hackers are now capable of perpetrating large-scale data breaches that leave hundreds of thousands—and in many cases tens of millions—of individuals at risk of identity theft,"[37] says Rita Glavin, head of the Justice Department's criminal division.

"Skilled hackers are now capable of perpetrating large-scale data breaches that leave hundreds of thousands—and in many cases tens of millions—of individuals at risk of identity theft."[37]

— Rita Glavin, head of the Justice Department's criminal division.

Determining exact numbers is difficult, however. Many companies do not report hacking incidents because they fear such reports will alarm their customers or damage their reputation with shareholders or investors. This makes it difficult to track the exact number of data breaches. Small businesses are especially vulnerable because they usually have unguarded access to customer credit card records, employee payroll files, and other information. Most do not use or keep access logs, so even if their information has been stolen, they probably will not know it.

They are by no means the only targets for hackers. According to the Government Accountability Office:

> Data breaches have occurred across a range of entities, including federal, state, and local government agencies; retailers; financial institutions; colleges and universities; and medical facilities. Breaches have varied in size and have resulted from both criminal actions and accidental incidents. Most of the breaches reported in the news media have involved data that included personal identifiers such as SSNs, while others have involved only account information such as credit card numbers.[38]

Millions Affected

A major breach occurred in March 2011 when hackers broke into Texas-based Epsilon, a firm that facilitates e-mail for more than twenty-five hundred companies worldwide. The company handles up to 40 billion e-mails annually, and some of its well-known clients include Best Buy, JPMorgan Chase, Citi, Walgreens, Capital One, and the College Board. While no sensitive information was taken—the hackers were only able to obtain the names and e-mails of individual customers of the companies that were affected —experts warned that those customers were likely to receive an increased number of spam and phishing e-mails as a result of the breach. The Identity Theft Assistance Center called the Epsilon breach one of the six worst of 2011, noting that conservative estimates indicated that 60 million customer e-mail addresses were exposed. "Epsilon has not disclosed the names of the companies affected or the total number of names stolen," notes the Privacy Rights Clearinghouse, which tracks data breaches. "However, millions of customers received notices from a growing list of companies, making this the largest security breach ever."[39]

Another major attack occurred in early March 2012, when hackers broke into the system of Global Payments of Atlanta. The firm serves as an intermediary between merchants and credit card

Unhacked Data Breaches

Sometimes data breaches occur without hackers. In 2010 three state agencies in Texas—with a total of 3.5 million records that included Social Security numbers—transferred databases to the state comptroller's office. Despite long-standing practice, the three agencies did not encrypt the data. The problem was compounded when the comptroller's office also failed to follow its own system of checks and balances. The data were supposed to be encrypted, placed on a secure server, then deleted after seven days.

As a result of the twin failures, the information was easily available on a server that was accessible to the public for nearly a year. When authorities discovered the mistake, they moved the data to a secure location. The employees responsible for the error were fired. The comptroller's office contacted the Texas attorney general and FBI to investigate whether any data had been misused. Astonishingly, there was no indication that it had. "I deeply regret the exposure of the personal information that occurred and am angry that it happened," said Comptroller Susan Combs. "I want to reassure people that the information was sealed off from any public access immediately after the mistake was discovered and was then moved to a secure location."

Quoted in Matt Leibowitz, "Data Breach Exposes 3.5 Million Social Security Numbers," *Security News Daily*, April 12, 2011. www.securitynewsdaily.com.

companies Visa, MasterCard, American Express, and Discover. When a merchant swipes a credit card, the information—account number, expiration date, and cardholder name—first goes to Global or similar companies, where it is processed. Then the processor connects with the credit card company and passes along the data. In turn, the data is forwarded to the card-issuing bank, which authorizes payment. "Hackers are well aware that these [processing] systems don't have the same sophisticated levels of security as the banks," says Tom Kellerman, an officer at a computer security company. "The payment processors have become [the banks'] Achilles' heel."[40]

While the card companies were not directly affected, authorities believe that between 1 million and 3 million accounts may have been exposed. The companies said they would reissue cards for those whose accounts were compromised.

One-Stop Identity Shopping

In many if not most cases, hackers do not use the information they obtain themselves. Instead, they sell it on what has become a flourishing worldwide network of illegal trading sites where the information may be easily bought and sold. The thieves maintain shopping sites that mimic those of reputable retailers. For example, the credit report belonging to an Illinois man born in 1976 with a credit score of 705 (which is considered good) is worth seventy-five dollars. Another Illinois man, born three years earlier, has an even better credit score of 805, which is nearing a perfect score of 850. His report goes for ninety dollars. The final column is the familiar "Add to Cart" and has a link for easy ordering. "It shows how people with good credit and a net worth now have a bull's-eye on their backs,"[41] says Dan Clements, who operates CloudEyes.com, an Internet security company.

> "People with good credit and a net worth now have a bull's-eye on their backs."[41]
>
> — Dan Clements, Internet security company official.

Many of these sites also offer handy tips for more effective hacking. Some include a rating system—somewhat similar to Amazon's customer comments on their purchases—where members can post feedback on the quality of stolen credit card numbers and other information offered for sale. And many will accept requests for specific types of stolen information and will also sell complete phishing websites and e-mail templates so that even absolute beginners can easily run phishing scams. In one variation on this theme some hackers have employed what is known as "PIN cashing." They send stolen financial information—including PINs—to criminals around the world, who promptly go to ATM machines and make withdrawals.

Who Are the Hackers?

The identity of hackers varies widely. Some come from organized crime. Russia, with an estimated six thousand street gangs, has been identified as a particularly fertile field. Authorities believe that many of those gangs are involved in identity theft. Some of these enterprises operate on a massive scale. As *BusinessWeek* writer Brian Grow notes, "Today's cybercrooks are becoming ever more tightly organized. Like the Mafia, hacker groups have virtual godfathers to map strategy, capos to issue orders, and soldiers to do the dirty

Some hackers use their skills to publicize stances on political or social issues while others appear to have altogether different motives. One 2012 hacking attack potentially exposed up to 3 million credit card accounts.

work. Their *omertà*, or vow of silence, is made easier by the anonymity of the Web. And like legit businesses, they're going global."[42]

The talent pool of hackers is seemingly inexhaustible. Many of them are small-time cons who mine the Internet for the abundance of freely available instruction in the hacking trade. As the website PrivacyMatters.com points out,

> Any petty criminal can now learn how to become an accomplished hacker free of charge, and possibly earn a much better living for a lot less risk. The criminals who used to lurk in doorways armed with a crowbar now lurk in front of laptops armed with a chai latte. These guys know that it's much easier to break into a business through the Internet to commit identity theft than through a skylight, and there's no chance of being bitten by the owner's Doberman.[43]

Other hackers are disgruntled former employees. For example, a man who left a small New York software company used a password that had not been canceled to steal more than thirty thousand credit reports over a two-year period and sell them for thirty dollars each. His crime cost the company an estimated $100 million.

Anonymous Makes Headlines

In the past few years, a loose network of hackers called Anonymous has made headlines for their attacks, most of which are socially and politically motivated. But on Christmas Day 2011, Anonymous turned its attention to Stratfor, a company that provides strategic intelligence on global business, economics, security, and geopolitical affairs. The hackers posted a list that not only revealed Stratfor's confidential client list—which included the United Nations, Lockheed Martin, and the Defense Department—but also credit card details for four thousand clients. The group noted that it also had details of nearly one hundred thousand additional credit card accounts. The hackers further boasted that they had used the information to make more than a million dollars in charitable donations. However, that part of the strategy may have backfired. Cardholders could easily cancel the donations, and the charities could be hit with penalties and fees for reversing the charges.

The incident also seemed intended to embarrass Stratfor. Several clients were in New Zealand, and local technology commentator Colin Jackson said, "The government departments and (New Zealand) companies . . . are going to have to go around and get those credit cards stopped, and decide whether to continue dealing with this outfit Stratfor. Stratfor has made a press statement saying 'oh, this kind of thing happens to everybody and it's pretty hard to keep these guys out.' Yeah, right, well, you are supposed to be security experts."[44]

Two months earlier, Anonymous had embarrassed a number of police departments and related organizations in support of the Occupy Movement that had attracted significant media attention in the United States. One of their primary targets was the Boston Police Department, which the hackers accused of aggression and brutality against the demonstrators. Anonymous members claimed that they "hacked, defaced, and destroyed several law enforcement targets, leaking over 600MB [megabytes] of private information including internal documents, membership rosters, addresses, passwords, Social Security numbers, and other confidential data."[45]

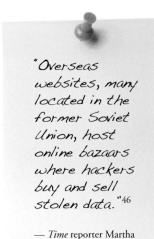

"Overseas websites, many located in the former Soviet Union, host online bazaars where hackers buy and sell stolen data."[46]

— *Time* reporter Martha C. White.

Hijacking Entire Credit Reports

Some hackers branched out beyond credit cards and, in an operation that came to light in 2012, stole entire credit reports. These are detailed summaries of an individual's credit history and personal data. They are prepared by credit bureaus and used by lenders to determine the creditworthiness of a loan applicant. As *Time* reporter Martha C. White writes, "Overseas websites, many located in the former Soviet Union, host online bazaars where hackers buy and sell stolen data. They also swap tips for cracking into supposedly secure systems like CreditReport.com, a site owned by credit bureau Experian, and AnnualCreditReport.com, which is overseen by the Federal Trade Commission."[46]

These report sites are guarded by a series of challenge questions that employ a multiple-choice format. However, most sites use

The Two Sides of Hacking

One of the first major data breaches came in 1999, when nineteen-year-old Welsh computer student Raphael Gray hacked into several e-commerce websites, stole up to twenty-six thousand credit card numbers, and posted some of them on the Internet. Gray adopted the nickname of *Curador*, which is Portuguese for "custodian." He also called himself the "Saint of e-commerce" and insisted that his primary motivation was to expose the weaknesses of a Microsoft security product. He even claimed to have used company cofounder Bill Gates's number to send him some prescription drugs. Judge Gareth Davies took a different view of Gray's handiwork: "You caused great expense and inconvenience—running into hundreds of thousands of pounds. It is fortunate no-one took advantage of the information you put on the net." Many cardholders had to cancel their cards, and several websites were crippled. The total estimated damage exceeded $3 million. Though prosecutors talked publicly about seeking jail time for Gray, he managed to escape going to prison. Instead he had to undergo three years of psychiatric treatment. "I would do it all again but another time I would choose to ensure that I acted legally," he said.

Quoted in BBC News, "Teen Hacker Escapes Jail Sentence," July 6, 2001. http://news.bbc.co.uk.

the same set of questions, so determined hackers can deduce the answers by a process of elimination. Some hackers even provide step-by-step instructions for their customers. The upshot is that—given those instructions and a little bit of research—it is often just as easy for thieves to answer the questions as it is for the victims themselves. Social media sites facilitate this research. "The information people are disclosing is not the entire piece of the puzzle but it's certainly helpful," says Thomas Oscherwitz of ID Analytics, a consumer risk management company. "Thieves steal identities in pieces and layer them on each other for a clearer picture."[47]

Stolen credit reports provide a wealth of personal background information. This information allows the thieves to open a plethora of new accounts in the victims' names. Worried about the financial risks this poses, some victims end up paying significant amounts of money for credit freezes—which stipulate that credit information cannot be released or sold to merchants or financial agencies without the consent of the victim. As Martha C. White adds, "What's scariest about this is that crooks aren't hacking company networks, like the data breach with Visa and MasterCard third-party processor Global Payments. . . . They're exploiting the security loopholes of legitimate websites—one of which is overseen by a government regulatory agency—that are operated by the bureaus which have built an enormous business out of cataloging and quantifying every detail of our financial histories."[48]

A Case Study in Hacking

Sometimes hackers are caught and prosecuted. In 2010 twenty-eight-year-old Albert Gonzalez was sentenced to twenty years in prison for hacking schemes that had lasted for nearly ten years and resulted in the theft of as many as 130 million credit and debit cards. When he was indicted the previous year, it marked the largest data breach indictment brought by the US Justice Department. As US attorney Ralph J. Marra Jr. said at the time, "This investigation marks the continued success of law enforcement in tracking down cutting edge hacking schemes committed by hackers working together across the globe."[49]

And the sentence itself was the longest ever handed down for such a crime. As far as the government was concerned, the punishment was fully deserved. In the words of the chief prosecutor in Gonzalez's case, "The sheer extent of the human victimization caused by Gonzalez and his organization is unparalleled."[50]

Apart from the sheer magnitude of the theft and the sentence, what made the Gonzalez case especially interesting was that for several years he was working for the government at the same time he and his associates were ripping off the accounts of some of the

largest and best-known retailers and banks in the United States. Law enforcement had known him since he was twelve and had hacked into NASA computers. After being arrested ten years later, he agreed to work with the Secret Service as a paid informant in order to stay out of prison.

Operation Firewall

Gonzalez helped to put together a sting operation called Operation Firewall against ShadowCrew, one of the most notorious rings of cybercriminals. Founded in 2002, in just two years ShadowCrew was a sprawling network of at least four thousand members based on four continents who committed e-commerce mayhem. A federal prosecutor called ShadowCrew "an eBay, Monster.com and Myspace for cybercrime."[51] After months of painstaking efforts, Gonzalez coordinated a chat session that had most of the leaders

The hacker group Anonymous has made headlines mostly for politically and socially motivated attacks. As in this image from a 2012 online video, the group is often represented by a person wearing a Guy Fawkes mask. Fawkes was part of a plot to blow up the English Parliament in London in 1605.

at their computers simultaneously so they could be rounded up at the same time. Twenty-eight in eight states and six countries were arrested, with nineteen eventually being indicted. Many authorities regard it as the most successful government cybercrime operation ever carried out.

However, Gonzalez wanted to put the knowledge he had gained during Operation Firewall to use for his own profit. He had been especially struck by how vulnerable WiFi was as companies rushed to take advantage of that technology. According to *New York Times* reporter James Verini, "Gonzalez was especially intrigued by the possibilities of a technique known as 'war driving': hackers would sit in cars or vans in the parking lots of big-box stores with laptops and high-power radio antennae and burrow through companies' vulnerable WiFi networks. Adepts [skilled hackers] could get into a billion-dollar multinational's servers in minutes."[52]

Within a few months, Gonzalez had gained access to more than 40 million credit cards. At the same time he had put together an international organization that spanned much of the same territory within which ShadowCrew had operated. With millions of dollars pouring in, he also devoted considerable time to developing a sophisticated system of money-laundering.

After his arrest he explained the appeal of what he was doing. "At first I did it for monetary reasons. The service's salary wasn't enough, and I needed the money. By then I'd already created the snowball and had to keep doing it. I wanted to quit but couldn't. . . . Whatever morality I should have been feeling was trumped by the thrill."[53] He even coined a name for what he was doing: Operation Get Rich or Die Tryin', after rapper 50 Cent's album and film.

As his operation expanded, along with his millions of dollars in earnings, he stopped working for the government. By then several large companies he had attacked were frantically enlisting federal help for massive data breaches. Although he had been careful, he had not been careful enough. A chance arrest led agents to Gonzalez, who was taken into custody in May 2008 and eventually pleaded guilty at his trial. At the minimum, Gonzalez and his associates infiltrated at least five hundred banks. Legal fees and reimbursements directly connected to their activities totaled more than $400 million. And the damage was probably even worse. "The majority of the stuff I hacked was never brought into public light,"[54] said one of Gonzalez's top aides.

Pulling the Plug on PlayStation

Not all hackers go after obvious financial data. On April 20, 2011, a notice on Sony's PlayStation Network (PSN) blog notified its users that the network itself and the Qriocity service—which the console requires for multiplayer activities—were out of commission. The following day, another post revealed that it might be another day or two before service was restored. A third revealed an "external intrusion" and that the systems had been taken offline to shore them up against this intrusion.

A few days later came the real bombshell. As technology reporter Jared Newman said,

> Sony's Playstation Network outage has gone from one of the worst Internet service interruptions ever to one of the worst security failures in consumer electronics history. If you're one of the 70 million members of the Playstation Network or Qriocity services, all of your personal and log-in information is compromised. Everything. That includes your name, address, e-mail address, birthday, user name and password. Your profile data, purchase history and password security answers may be compromised as well.[55]

While Sony said it had no evidence of the loss of credit card information, it could not rule out the possibility. At the very least, the company urged PlayStation customers to change their passwords, keep an eye on upcoming credit card statements, and be alert to the likelihood of postal and e-mail scams.

Sony may have unintentionally contributed to the situation. "Notably, these breaches occurred after Sony had laid off many of its security personnel in the months preceding the attacks," noted the Privacy Rights Clearinghouse. "Ultimately, Sony faced an ongoing customer relations fallout—as well as class-action lawsuits—over its failure to protect user records."[56]

Whether through corporate missteps or their own determined

efforts, hackers account for a significant increase in the rate of identity theft, usually targeting institutions that oversee millions of records. Their efforts can be especially disheartening to people who have made significant personal efforts to avoid phishers and other information thieves yet find themselves victimized through no fault of their own.

Facts

- ShadowCrew's founders were Andrew Mantovani, a part-time community college student, and David Appleyard, a onetime mortgage broker.

- In January 2012 Twitter users fell for a phishing scam that began "something funny about you." The scammers used Twitter usernames and passwords to send spam to the followers of the compromised users.

- In one case of PIN cashing, the thieves made nine thousand withdrawals totaling $5 million in less than forty-eight hours.

- Some hackers have "joint ventures," in which other network members use stolen numbers to buy goods. The goods are sold and proceeds shared among the participants.

- According to the Ponemon Institute, data breach incidents cost about $200 per compromised record in terms of lost business, legal fees, and other expenses.

Can Identity Theft Be Prevented?

I s it possible to eliminate identity theft? Given its long history and the relative ease with which identities can be compromised, the answer is almost certainly no. Nevertheless, it does seem possible to reduce its incidence and severity. Any program to reduce identity theft has several components. One is greater enforcement of existing laws and the possible addition of new ones. Another is increased vigilance by financial institutions and other corporations that maintain sensitive personal data and the application of greater safeguards to that data. A third is education, making individuals aware of the steps they can take to keep their identities safe.

Identity Theft Laws

When identity theft began emerging as an issue in the digital age, Congress responded by passing the Identity Theft and Assumption Deterrence Act. Under the provisions of the 1998 law, identity theft became a federal crime. It recognized as the victim the person whose identity had been stolen rather than the financial institutions that held the credit cards or bank accounts of that individual. The law called for penalties of up to 15 years in prison (though in reality sentences were usually much lower) and fines of up to $250,000. But as Jo Alison Taylor of the University of Alabama law school pointed out not long after the law was passed, "Unfortunately, the number of cases is so large that investigations and prosecutions are rare unless the loss is very large."[57]

So despite the new law, police and prosecutors still spent a lot less time and energy on identity theft than on other, more conventional crimes. This hampered prevention efforts. Congressman John Carter of Texas, a former county judge, sought to remedy this problem when he sponsored the Identity Theft Penalty Enhancement Act, which Congress passed in 2004. The act created the new crime of "aggravated identity theft," which added two more mandatory years to prison sentences for those convicted of identity theft. As Carter said at the time of its passage: "Identity theft was basically being ignored. There's a reality in how prosecutors do their business and that reality is that they're going to take the cases that are easiest to prove and carry the most weight."[58]

Politicians at other levels of government also began to take an interest in preventing identity theft. In 2006 President George W. Bush established the President's Task Force on Identity Theft. Led by the attorney general and chairman of the Federal Trade Commission, members included the heads of fifteen government departments. The task force issued its Strategic Plan the following year, which included thirty-one recommendations to combat identity theft. In 2008 it released a list of steps that had actually been implemented, such as mailing identity theft protection information to nearly 150 million individuals and businesses and coordinating programs to provide free legal assistance to victims.

Despite these efforts, identity theft continued to increase. In 2010, inspector general Glenn Fine of the US Department of Justice (DOJ), issued a report indicating that efforts to combat the problem had been relatively ineffectual. In some cases Task Force recommendations had been ignored. The report states, "We . . . found that to some degree identity theft initiatives have faded as priorities. In addition, we found that DOJ has not developed a coordinated plan to combat identity theft separate from the recommendations of the President's Task Force ."[59]

Another federal law provides protection for foster children, who are vulnerable to identity theft because of the number of people who see paperwork that includes their personal information. Congress passed the Child and Family Services Improvement and Innovation Act in September 2011. One of the bill's provisions mandates an annual free credit report for foster children sixteen and over and assistance in clearing up any inaccuracies. The website of the bill's sponsor, Representative Jim Langevin of Rhode Island, notes that "current practices put foster children at a greatly increased risk of having their personal information compromised because their Social Security numbers and other identifying records pass through many hands. Langevin's broader legislation would end the use of the Social Security number as an identifier for foster children."[60]

Changes in Social Security

Several recent changes in the usage and issuance of Social Security numbers are intended to cut down on their theft. The Social Security Protection Act of 2010 forbids government agencies from printing SSNs on checks and allowing prisoners of any

Recent changes in federal laws and policies are aimed at reducing the likelihood of identity theft. They call for more cautious use of Social Security numbers and new ways of creating the numbers.

jurisdiction—federal, state, or local—from having access to SSNs of other individuals. "Social Security numbers are among Americans' most valuable but vulnerable assets," says California senator Dianne Feinstein, one of the bill's sponsors. "Identity theft is a serious concern for all consumers, and we should make every effort to protect personal information."[61]

In another significant move, the SSA began making all nine digits random for new accounts starting in 2011. "As the SSN is increasingly used by public and private entities in conjunction with other tools and processes for identity verification, instances of SSN fraud, misuse, and identity theft are also on the rise," the SSA explains. "SSN randomization will help protect an individual's SSN by making it more difficult to reconstruct an SSN using public information."[62]

Defense Department Gets Involved

In yet another proactive move, the Department of Defense is removing SSNs from military ID cards and replacing them with two new numbers: a general identification number and another that can be used to claim and verify benefits. Under this program, which began in 2008, ID cards for active-duty military are being replaced with the new ones as they expire. Defense Department officials anticipate that the changeover will be completed by 2015.

Because of the number of places in which servicemen and women have to put their numbers—dogtags, duffle bags, clothing, and so forth—they are especially at risk for identity theft. In addition, military personnel face problems most identity theft victims do not have to confront. As one serviceman told Congress during hearings on the proposed changes,

"Identity theft is a serious concern for all consumers, and we should make every effort to protect personal information."[61]

— US senator Dianne Feinstein.

While I am concerned about myself, I am even more concerned for those 19-year-old soldiers and their families that are so easily victimized by this crime. Imagine their spouses, new to the way of the military, trying to balance the day-to-day challenges of a young family, with the crippling effects of identity theft. Furthermore, I am concerned because I can see how it could be nearly impossible to fight identity theft problems from another part of the world.[63]

State Laws

In addition to federal efforts, every state has laws regarding identity theft. In general, the provisions are similar to those on the federal level, though there may be some differences. For example, in Illinois aggravated identity theft involves victims aged sixty or over, disabled persons, or acts committed in furtherance of gang activities. If the value of the theft exceeds $100,000, conviction carries a prison term of six to thirty years without possibility of parole. And California has passed legislation tightening the granting of credit. Previously only an SSN match was required. Now, credit grantors in the state must match three identifiers from credit applications to those on file at the credit bureau before they issue credit, thereby reducing the number of fraudulent applications.

Members of the military have traditionally been identified by Social Security numbers on paperwork, dog tags (pictured), clothing, and other personal items. Under new policies, Social Security numbers will be replaced with other identifiers to help guard against identity theft.

Some states have data breach notification laws, which require any organization that suffers a breach to notify that state's affected residents. The data breach laws in Massachusetts are regarded as among the nation's toughest. Organizations that store personal information of Massachusetts residents must encrypt that data or face fines or lawsuits. Since state laws regarding data breach reporting vary so much, one of the recommendations of the President's Task Force on Identity Theft was the establishment of a single federal standard. Legislation introduced into the US Senate to establish such a standard in 2011, however, became bogged down in partisan arguments.

In 2012 Maryland took a major step toward protecting children's credit with the Maryland Identity Child Lock bill. Prior to its passage, credit agencies could refuse to put a credit freeze on a person with no credit history—such as young children. Now, under the terms of this bill, when parents or guardians ask for a credit freeze on their children, the request must be granted. The freeze prevents a potential thief from obtaining credit in their name.

More Security Measures Needed

Laws alone are not enough to eliminate or significantly reduce identity theft. Many security experts say that banks and credit card companies are not doing enough to safeguard customer information. For example, many people criticize banks for their continued use of SSNs as authenticators, especially in dealing with customer service representatives. "Just exposing it to the customer service rep, that's a weakness in itself," says Tim Rohrbaugh, vice president of information security at Intersections, a risk management company for the financial services industry. "By introducing another pair of eyes being able to view that data, that in and of itself is an unnecessary weakness."[64] Even the common practice of asking for just the last four digits of the SSN can compromise security, as those are the digits chosen at random and therefore the hardest for would-be thieves to obtain.

On the other hand, many banks have increased their customer education efforts. Some prominently post notices on their websites that they never request personal information via e-mail or

Adapting to Changing Conditions

A New Jersey case demonstrates how states are dealing with new situations involving identity theft and expanding its definition under the law. In 2007 a woman named Dana Thornton dated police detective Michael Lasalandra for several months. After the couple broke up, the embittered Thornton set up a Facebook account in his name. Writing as if she were Lasalandra, she made statements such as "I'm a sick piece of scum with a gun" and posted numerous incidents of his supposed bad behavior. These purported to involve drugs and excessive use of alcohol, in addition to unflattering pictures. She was charged with identity theft.

At first she was defiant. Her lawyer said that "In New Jersey no courts have ever ruled that creating a profile of anyone online, without the individual's consent, constitutes false impersonation." He asked that the charges be dismissed.

Late in 2011 Judge David Ironson refused to dismiss the charges. He ruled that New Jersey's identity theft laws do apply to electronic media. Soon afterward, Thornton agreed to enter a diversion program—a combination of counseling and community service—in which the charges would be dropped when she completed it.

Quoted in Tom Jacobs, "Is a Fake Facebook Page Identity Theft?," askthejudge.info, January 12, 2012. www.askthejudge.info.

Quoted in Matt Liebowitz, "Facebook Case Tests Identity Theft Laws," *Security News Daily*, October 27, 2011. www.msnbc.msn.com.

send messages requesting patrons to click on links to provide that information. They may also offer samples of fraudulent e-mails to further educate customers. This information helps to counter authentic-looking but otherwise bogus e-mails.

Some credit card companies take careful note of the way their cards are used and will automatically refuse to authorize charges if there is doubt about their authenticity. In a recent case, a Washington State man received a phone call from his credit card issuer regarding a charge of less than $100 from a company in the Netherlands. The man told the issuer that he had never been in the Netherlands and had not charged anything that might have originated there. The card company rejected the charge and issued new cards to him and his family.

Corporate Security

Corporations may be especially vulnerable to identity theft. According to some estimates, up to 75 percent of workplace identity thefts are committed by employees. There are several areas of vulnerability. Employees in Human Resources may have especially easy access to sensitive information, which they can use themselves or sell. Other employees may find it easy to hack into employee records. Even janitors can uncover potentially useful information by going through trash at night and finding documents carelessly thrown aside.

Critics of corporate security maintain that many corporations do not do enough to screen prospective employees, and many take too long to deny fired/separated employees access to company information. In addition, they say that temporary employees who have access to sensitive data may not be subject to sufficient screening. Also many companies—financial and otherwise—may outsource sensitive functions and have little or no idea what their contractor's security procedures are.

Learning to Live More Safely

Consumers cannot depend solely on laws, banks, and other businesses to prevent identity theft. As Frank Abagnale notes, "Identity thieves—the professionals, at least—spend all their time trying to outwit you so they can steal your money, while you spend at most a small portion of your time trying to keep them from getting it. So the odds distinctly favor them. But you can reduce those percentages significantly if you take a number of fairly simple precautions."[65]

ATM Safety

Thieves using skimming devices on Automated Teller Machines (ATMs) have been able to access bank accounts. In one case, perpetrators compromised more than forty ATMs and netted over $1.5 million dollars between May 2011 and January 2012. Experts offer some tips on ways to keep personal banking information private. Some clues to recognizing skimmers on ATMs are a difference in color from the rest of the machine or some kind of fastening device such as tape or wire. More brazen thieves might put the skimmer in plain sight with a notice that users should insert the card there first.

Some experts advocate using the same ATM machine if possible, which makes it easier to spot any changes resulting from tampering, and carefully examining any unfamiliar ATMs before use. Many suggest using ATMs directly connected with banks—preferably inside the building—rather than ones at convenience stores, gas stations, and similar locations, which may be less secure and more likely to be subject to tampering.

Users should also be vigilant against "shoulder surfing," a situation in which someone standing nearby and feigning disinterest is actually carefully watching potential victims as they type in their PINs. Their next step is to steal the card, usually through traditional ways such as purse snatching. In a matter of moments the thieves can quickly access sensitive accounts. For added ATM security, experts suggest covering the keypad with the free hand.

Many experts agree that the most important way consumers can protect themselves is to continually monitor credit reports, both their own and their children's (even if the children have no credit). Some even suggest this be done every three months. Along the same lines, people should keep track of credit card billing cycles and carefully check monthly statements for any unfamiliar charges. Since most banks now make it possible for their customers to monitor their accounts online, it only takes a minute or two each day to check for any unusual withdrawals.

Consumers also need to be as sparing as possible with giving out their SSNs. While many forms routinely include a space for the SSN, in many cases it is not required. For example, the payroll department of a new employer needs it. So does a bank. A grocery store club card does not. As James Munton and Jelita McLeod observe, "When in doubt, don't provide it, and see if they come back to you for it. If they do, ask why they need it. This is YOUR information. You are not obligated to share it with anyone if they cannot provide sufficient proof that they need it."[66] People also need to be especially wary of giving it out to strangers on the telephone or via e-mail. And they should never carry their Social Security card in their wallet (because of the possibility that the wallet could be stolen or lost).

Prevention also entails protecting one's computer. Maintaining antivirus and antimalware software and continually updating it is key for computer protection. So is deleting questionable e-mails, especially those that contain links, without clicking on the link. Any time that someone gets rid of a computer, it is imperative to make sure that the hard drive is wiped clean.

Another aspect of prevention is being mindful of where and how online purchases are made. Authorities offer several online buying tips. They include using one credit card for purchases (which makes monitoring easier), not using public computers for purchases because it is impossible to know whether these computers are secure, and making sure to shop only on trustworthy sites. These sites can be recognized by the https:// that begins the URL (the *s* is added) and a padlock symbol in the lower right corner of the browser window.

Experts also urge people to get into the habit of using a shredder for anything that might reveal sensitive information, such as preapproved credit card invitations and old bank or credit card statements. The smaller the particles the shredder produces, the better. Some shredders simply slice documents into long strips which can be reassembled.

Secure Passwords

Another key to preventing ID theft involves the use of carefully chosen passwords and PINs and continually safeguarding them. A 2012 survey of businesses revealed that the most common password was "Password1." According to Microsoft's Active Directory identity management software, this password has three desirable elements: It has an upper-case letter, a number, and nine characters. Yet it might take a hacker all of five minutes to figure it out. CNNMoney security writer Stacy Cowley says,

> Adding complexity to your password—swapping 'password' for 'p@S$w0rd'—protects against so-called 'dictionary' attacks, which automatically check against a list of standard words. But attackers are increasingly using brute-force tools that simply cycle through all possible character combinations. Length is the only effective guard against those. A seven-character password has 70 trillion possible combinations; an eight-character password takes that to more than 6 quadrillion.[67]

Length is just one consideration in creating a strong password. The actual characters used are also important. Experts suggest avoiding birthdays, names of pets, significant accomplishments, nicknames, and so on because these are relatively easy for thieves to guess if they have even a little information about the person. For ease in remembering, some experts suggest picking something personally meaningful but unknown to anyone else and—since many passwords have to include a combo of numbers and letters—adding a number at the end. Experts disagree, though, on how many passwords people should have. Some recommend using one very complex (to anyone else) password, while others advocate using different ones for every site. Either way, most experts advocate changing them regularly.

There are numerous methods of choosing a good password. One method begins with an easy-to-remember phrase, such as one

"Adding complexity to your password— swapping 'password' for 'p@S$word'— protects against so-called 'dictionary' attacks, which automatically check against a list of standard words."[67]

— CNNMoney security writer Stacy Cowley.

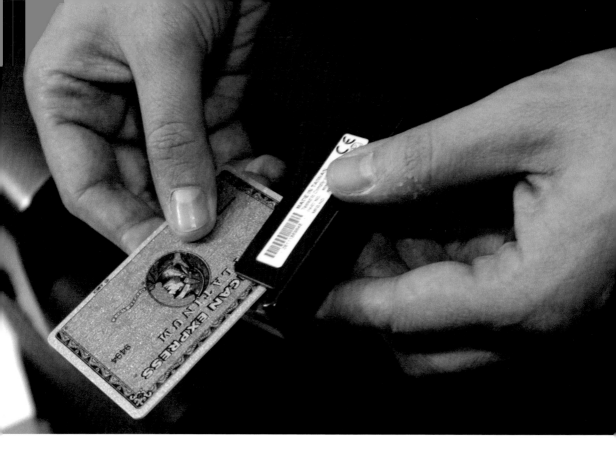

of the common mnemonics for the planets and their order (Mercury, Venus, Earth, Mars, Jupiter, Saturn, Uranus, Neptune): My Very Energetic Mother Jumps Skateboards Under Narnia. Then add special characters, punctuation, numbers and capitalization. The resulting password might be something like mv2$em,JS@un6. Another method is selecting three unrelated short words (rat, sun, and free) and linking them: rAt&6sun*!FreE9.

Protecting Plastic

Credit cards used to make public purchases at places such as retail stores and restaurants are also one of the favorite targets of identity thieves, who employ a technique called skimming to obtain card numbers and then fraudulently use them. Skimming involves inserting a device that "reads" the card's magnetic strip into the slot of a legitimate device or using small handheld skimmers which can be purchased relatively inexpensively on the Internet. The data is then downloaded onto a computer and can be e-mailed anywhere.

To obtain the three- or four-digit security number on the reserve side of the card, the person handling the transaction merely flips it over on the pretext of checking the customer's signature and adds it to the data. Creating a new card with the stolen number is a relatively simple matter. The thieves then go on shopping sprees with those cards, typically buying high-end merchandise they sell to unsuspecting customers who may not ask many questions about where the items came from in the first place.

Abagnale dismisses the notion that the more upscale the establishment, the less likely that someone will become victimized. "Don't think that because you're shopping or eating at an expensive place with rave reviews, the sales help can't possibly be skimming cards," he notes. "[Identity thieves] want the big spenders with big credit, not the patrons of the greasy spoon or the Dollar Store."[68]

Skimming is especially prevalent in restaurants and bars, particularly when the waitperson presents diners with the bill, then disappears for a few moments to swipe the card after the cardholder signs it. Therefore, Abagnale and other security experts recommend that cardholders never let their card go out of sight. They can either pay the bill at the front desk or, in some cases, the waitperson can scan the card at the table. This measure also prevents a variation of skimming, in which a waitperson makes a quick photocopy of the card for potentially illegal purposes. They also urge cardholders to retain copies of all purchase receipts and compare them with the monthly statements.

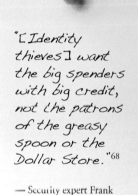

"[Identity thieves] want the big spenders with big credit, not the patrons of the greasy spoon or the Dollar Store."[68]

— Security expert Frank Abagnale.

Playing Catch-Up

In a sense, preventing identity theft is a game of catch-up. The thieves were the first ones out of the starting gate, and everything that has happened since then in the way of prevention is a reaction to this early lead. Facebook provides a case in point. As Ondrej Krehel notes, Facebook's extreme popularity makes it "the preferred platform for hackers and scammers." Bogus newsfeeds are a fertile field for downloading malware. Another is free items for Farmville and similar games. And as the Osama bin Laden example illustrates, so are shocking videos. So, Krehel continues, "It's no surprise that we're seeing a boom in security-centric Facebook apps, such as Safego, designed to halt malicious use of Facebook accounts."[69]

In other words, each new scam eventually is matched by a way of dealing with it—thereby setting off a search for a new scam. And at the same time, lawmakers at the state and federal levels and businesses that deal with sensitive information try to help deal with the situation. Unfortunately, however, identity theft is likely to remain a permanent part of the landscape. The best method of prevention is to remain constantly vigilant.

Facts

- Experts urge people never to post their exact birthdate and place of birth on social media sites.

- Facebook surveys such as "10 Things Others Don't Know About You" or "My Favorite Things," may serve as data-mining sites. ID thieves can also get password clues from questions such as the name of the street where people grew up or their favorite vacation spots.

- Putting sensitive mail in a mailbox and raising the flag may be an open invitation to thieves to steal it.

- One method of avoiding having to remember multiple complex passwords is to adopt one basic password, then add 1, 2, 3, and so on at the end for each different application.

- According to Internet security company McAfee, skimming from ATMs results in losses of more than $8.5 billion to consumers and companies annually. Some experts advise against the use of debit cards because if they are stolen, money from the victim's account can be immediately withdrawn and it can be difficult to get it back.

What Are the Challenges of Reclaiming a Stolen Identity?

Mari Frank was stunned one day in August 1996 when she received a phone call from a bank in Delaware. The bank asked her why she had not paid her $11,000 credit card bill. Frank had never heard of the bank. She did not have a credit card from that bank, and she had not made any of the charges that the bank was now demanding that she pay.

That phone call changed Frank's life. Because of it she became a pioneer in the fight against identity theft. At the time she received the call, hardly any resources were available for victims trying to deal with the problem. Her task was twofold: First she had to stop the financial bleeding, then she had to regain her stolen identity. In accomplishing this task, she blazed a trail that eventually helped many other people who were faced with the same situation. She would eventually become recognized as an authority on identity theft and even testify before the US Congress on several occasions.

Frank had no idea how the person who had stolen her identity had gained access to the personal information needed to open an account in her name with the Delaware bank. No one had stolen her wallet or robbed her. She was always careful with confidential documents that provided clues to her identity. After considerable

Around and Around We Go

The experience of a Connecticut woman—identified as Ms. X to preserve her privacy—illustrates the often frustrating nature of trying to recover from identity theft. When she was living in New Orleans in 2003, her apartment building supervisor's girlfriend stole her mail and fraudulently opened accounts in her name. She immediately filed a report with law enforcement in New Orleans. She was told they could do nothing, and they told her to deal directly with the credit bureaus. She moved to Connecticut and found out two years later that the thief had made nearly $5,000 in credit card charges in her name. She filed a report with her local police. They said the thief was now living in Arkansas and there was nothing they could do. Over the phone, she filed a third report with police in Fayetteville, Arkansas, who told her that they had identified the thief and even found documents in Ms. X's name. But the thief had fled before she could be arrested. Some time later, a fraudulent Chicago address turned up on Ms. X's credit report. She filed yet another report with Chicago police. It went nowhere.

The upshot is that despite following established procedures and filing timely police reports, Ms. X still had not completely regained her identity. Nevertheless, she urges victims to file police reports. "It may not help [police] make an arrest, but the report will convince companies that you aren't responsible for all those fraudulent charges on accounts you never opened," she says.

Quoted in John L. Fischer, "Outcome: Rolling the Dice with ID Restoration," CreditFYI. www.creditfyi.com.

persuasion, the bank told her that the cardholder lived in Ventura, California, which was a four-hour drive from Frank's home. That information further deepened the mystery. Frank had never lived in Ventura or even visited the city. Though the bank promised to send her copies of the paperwork that the person had filled out to get the account, it did not. And rather than cooperate with Frank in trying to resolve the situation, the bank turned her account over to a collection agency. The collection agency began a series of threatening phone calls. In desperation, Frank contacted the Ventura Police Department.

Help from a Fellow Victim

Few police departments had any experience dealing with identity theft in the mid-1990s, and even if they did, even fewer had the resources to devote to this type of crime. In a stroke of luck for Frank, the head of the Ventura Police fraud unit had been an identity theft victim himself. He sympathized with her situation and sent officers to the address listed for the credit card.

The woman who answered the door said Frank was a friend of hers and had once lived there. When the officers relayed that conversation to Frank, she said the claims were untrue. The Ventura police continued to investigate the situation. They learned that the woman was on probation for shoplifting and obtained a search warrant. Inside the house, they found dozens of documents with Frank's name on them: billing statements, personal checks, business cards, a credit report, even a letter from a car rental company threatening a lawsuit for damages to a car that the impersonator had rented in Frank's name.

The woman was arrested and eventually convicted of felony fraud. She received no jail time; her sentence only required her to take part in a work-furlough program. Between the time of her arrest and when she actually entered the program, she continued to make purchases in Frank's name. And after leaving the work-furlough program, the woman moved to another state where, according to Frank, she soon found a new victim—and was arrested again.

In the meantime, Frank had to pick up the pieces of her life and finances. Over the period of nearly a year, she picked her way through uncharted territory. She spent an estimated five hundred hours on the telephone; wrote nearly one hundred certified letters to businesses, government agencies, and credit organizations; and paid

Experts urge identity theft victims to contact the three major credit reporting agencies and place fraud alerts on their credit card accounts. The agencies have also made efforts to help consumers protect themselves against fraud, as can be seen in this promotion from the credit agency Equifax.

out considerable amounts of money—to say nothing of lost earnings from her law practice while she was dealing with the situation. It was not an easy process. "At the same time that I was assisting the police, district attorney, and courts in prosecuting the fraud perpetrator, I was also overwhelmed by the task of cleaning up my destroyed credit," Frank writes. "Straightening all this out was a true ordeal, which depleted me physically, emotionally, and financially."[70]

Reclaiming Identity

Frank and others who work in the field of online security urge identity theft victims to immediately take certain steps to reclaim their compromised identities. Some of these steps are now fairly routine but even so they can take considerable amounts of time and money. "Because identity theft is a broad category that encompasses a wide range of crimes, the recovery process will differ in length and complexity, depending on the exact nature of the theft, the amount involved, and the timeline of events," note James Munton and Jelita McLeod. "It is important to remember, however, that recovery *is* possible, no matter how difficult the situation seems."[71]

Taking Immediate Steps

While the process of recovery is likely to be fairly lengthy and time-consuming and involve a number of different steps, experts in the field believe that victims need to do several things right away. In some cases, there are time limits. The first step is to close all existing accounts. It is likely that if one account has been compromised, others have, too.

There are three major credit reporting agencies—Equifax, Experian, and TransUnion. Victims need to contact all three and place fraud alerts—notices that creditors need to take precautions before opening new accounts and/or make changes to existing accounts—on their credit reports. Legally, if a victim contacts one agency, that agency is obligated to contact the other two. Experts say, however, that to make sure the information is actually passed along, victims should follow up and contact all three themselves. Victims need to request a copy of their current credit reports. A close examination will reveal how many inquiries have been made, giving an idea of how many times a thief has tried to set up credit in the victim's name.

One of the most important steps is filing a police report, which includes copies of all evidence the victim has gathered. The report is an essential element in some of the future steps victims will take to recover their identity. It is also a useful tool in future dealings with banks and merchants that might be aware of the fraud alerts. Some experts recommend carrying a copy of the first page of the report to prove that the victim is genuine and not the imposter. After filing the police report, victims can request copies of any evidence with their name on it that police turn up. If the thief's identity becomes known at some point, individuals should not try to make personal contact. While the vast majority of identity thieves are nonviolent, their behavior may be unpredictable. Even if there is no physical contact, thieves may turn the tables and stalk their victims, thereby adding to their troubles.

Victims should also file a complaint with the FTC. The complaint includes documentation of the theft, including a description (if known) of how the thief obtained access to the victim's information. While the FTC is not an investigative body and cannot resolve individual cases, the information in a complaint can help the organization detect overall patterns of identity theft. These patterns can be useful to the thousands of law enforcement agencies that can conduct investigations and prosecute offenders. The FTC complaint can also be attached to the police report as additional documentation.

Victims need to keep detailed written accounts of every phone call and other form of communication during the recovery process. Any written communication should be sent via certified mail to prove that it was actually transmitted and received. And although creditors and collection agencies often put pressure on victims for immediate payment, no payments should be made until disputes are resolved.

Of these steps, dealing with the police often proves the most challenging. As Frank notes, "Many police departments are reluctant to take reports because they don't have the time or resources to investigate."[72] Neal O'Farrell, executive director of the Identity Theft Council, concurs. "The number one complaint I hear from victims is the indifference from law enforcement to identity theft and its victims," he says. "And most police departments I work with admit that at best they investigate less than 1% of identity theft cases. Most police departments don't have the resources to investigate identity theft."[73]

> "Many police departments are reluctant to take reports because they don't have the time or resources to investigate."[72]
>
> — Identity theft victim and expert Mari Frank.

FACT Act

Increased awareness of identity theft led to passage of the federal Fair and Accurate Credit Transaction Act of 2003 (also known as the FACT Act). The act aims to shorten the process that victims need to pursue in order to recover from identity theft. It established requirements for consumer reporting agencies, creditors, and others to help remedy identity theft. To take advantage of its provisions, victims must have filed a police report.

The FACT Act also provides certain rights and privileges to victims of identity theft to help them correct the damage created by the theft. Some of its rights and privileges include one-call fraud alerts to consumer credit reporting agencies, access to all records showing transactions believed to be a result of identity theft, blocking information resulting from identity theft on consumer credit reports, and preventing creditors from selling debts to collection agencies after being notified that the debt is due to fraud. One of the most useful aspects of the FACT Act is access to a free consumer credit report from each of the three major credit bureaus annually. Savvy consumers can take advantage of this privilege to provide themselves with one credit report every four months. For example, they might order their Equifax report on January 1, Experian on May 1, and Transunion September 1, then follow the same schedule each succeeding year.

Some states offer further legal assistance in the form of identity theft passports. These can be presented to law enforcement agencies to keep the holders from being mistakenly arrested for crimes committed in their name. The passports may also be submitted to creditors and to consumer reporting agencies as an official means of disputing purchases made by identity thieves.

"For a year, I was going to at least a dozen courthouses to sit in front of a (justice of the peace) and get [the parking tickets] turned around."[74]

— Identity theft victim Patrick Guest.

The Thief Who Loved KFC

The case of Canadian Patrick Guest illustrates just how long it can take to reclaim one's identity. Guest's troubles began in 1990 when a thief stole his wallet. Two years later, Guest got a bill for a neck brace from a hospital, though he had no neck problems and had never been to the hospital. When he called police to report the situation, they wanted to arrest him for drunk driving, driving without insurance, and a stack of parking tickets—all of which had been committed by the thief in Guest's name. "To get [the tickets] squashed, I had to submit an affidavit—in person—to each courthouse. For a year, I was going to at least a dozen courthouses to sit in front of a (justice of the peace) and get them turned around,"[74]

Guest says. Guest's courthouse odyssey cost him $2,000 plus his travel time, and he needed eight years to completely clear his name.

In 2010 the nightmare resumed. Credit card companies began calling Guest about recent unpaid charges he had supposedly made. The majority of these charges involved thousands of dollars worth of fried chicken meals from KFC. A year and half later, police finally arrested the imposter who had plagued Guest's life for nearly two decades and charged him with multiple counts of identity theft.

A New Social Security Number?

Perhaps the most controversial aspect of reclaiming one's identity is whether to seek a new SSN. Although this might seem like a logical step, most identity theft experts advise against doing so. For starters, the SSA links the two numbers to compute the individual's retirement benefits. And it cautions that a new number is unlikely to solve all the victim's problems. "Other governmental agencies (such as the Internal Revenue Service and state motor vehicle agencies) and private businesses (such as banks and credit reporting companies) likely will have records under your old number," says an official publication of the SSA. "Also, because credit reporting companies use the number, along with other personal information, to identify your credit record, using a new number will not guarantee you a fresh start. This is especially true if your other personal information, such as your name and address, remains the same."[75]

In addition, starting out with a completely fresh credit history may make it more difficult to obtain credit. If credit is granted, it may be under unfavorable conditions such as higher interest rates or a reduced maximum line of credit. And as Frank notes, "a new Social Security number makes the victim look more suspicious to creditors because the prior number will show up in the credit reporting database with an alert."[76] A clean record associated with one Social Security number is linked to another one that has significant problems. At the very least, the individual will have to do considerable explaining—if the organization to which he or she is applying for credit will even bother to listen.

An Ohio man named Scott Lewis, whose identity became linked with an accused murderer, got a new SSN on the advice of a prosecutor. The advice backfired. "My credit records now appeared to have a fraudulent SSN and the alert could only be seen by the creditors and not myself," Lewis said. "Now I have problems making the transition between the numbers and have a great deal of trouble with my credit. Having changed my SSN now requires continual explanations and makes everyone suspicious of me. Furthermore I will never know until I retire if all of my benefits will transfer."[77]

The only identity theft victims who might benefit from getting a new SSN are young adults who have little or no credit history. For example, a young woman named Debbie—a victim of identity theft—says, "I had no work history and no credit cards of my

No Guarantees

Applying for a new Social Security number is no guarantee that it will be issued. The first inkling that Joe (last name withheld for privacy) of Brighton, Colorado, had that his identity had been stolen came in 2007 when he was eighteen and he received a notice from state tax officials informing him that he had a substantial back tax bill. That began a five-year struggle to resolve the situation. Eventually a state tax official said that Joe would need a new Social Security number to clear up the situation and even personally escorted him to the local Social Security office. But the Social Security Administration twice refused to grant Joe a new number, saying that his credit history had not been harmed because the identity thief had never actually used his number to obtain credit. "They're just waiting until his credit is ruined in order to help him? That just seems ridiculous and appalling to me," said an attorney for the family.

Alan Gathright, "Social Security Denies ID Theft Victim New Number," 7News, February 10, 2011. www.thedenverchannel.com.

own, and the thief was unable to get approved for any credit or loans. By the time I got everything cleared up, I was 22 years old, and, as I mentioned earlier, I had no work history or credit history at the time. I feel that this was a definite advantage in being able to get rid of the old SSN, because I was not losing anything personal to me; I had not yet begun to build my credit."[78]

Identity Theft Insurance

Another area of considerable discussion involves identity theft insurance, which is one of the newest and fastest-growing areas of the insurance industry and is currently offered by nearly all major companies and a number of smaller ones. Typically it will assist victims in regaining their identity and restoring their previous credit rating. Many companies will oversee filling out the required forms, while some offer credit reporting as part of the package. One of the primary attractions is that the premium costs usually are quite low.

Tom Wilkinson, a fifty-two-year-old disabled Massachusetts man, enthusiastically endorsed identity theft insurance after becoming the victim of a phishing scam. He and his wife struggled with recovering from the situation. "The best thing we had was this identity-theft recovery [insurance], and it was a blessing," he said. "They walked us through everything, as far as putting alerts on accounts, etc. I don't know what we would have done without them. Because this had never happened to us before. I didn't know what to do and how to go there. . . . You really need help."[79]

Not all experts agree about its value, however. They point out that most policies do not provide coverage if a family member is responsible for the theft. Some have significant deductible amounts that are larger than the amount the average person would spend on phone calls and letters to clear up the problem. A number of policies also may not cover legal fees, and policy holders are not commonly reimbursed for the time spent away from their jobs to resolve the issues involved in identity theft. Nor do the policies cover actual financial losses due to identity theft.

"I feel that this was a definite advantage in being able to get rid of the old SSN, because I was not losing anything personal to me; I had not yet begun to build my credit."[78]

— Identity theft victim Debbie.

The Bottom Line

The bottom line is that recovering from identity theft can be very costly in terms of actual monetary or other losses, in the amount of time it takes to reclaim one's identity, and in the residual psychological and emotional effects that linger after the process has been completed. As Frank observes, "Yes, you will recover from having been robbed of your identity; just know, however, that a part of you may never be the same. . . . Figuratively speaking, you'll always be looking over your shoulder."[80]

A Cooperative Effort

Identity theft in the digital age is a serious and continuing problem. Some people talk about eliminating the crime of identity theft. But no one has been able to eliminate other crimes, such as murder and robbery. So to believe that society will ever be rid of the crime of identity theft might be unrealistic.

Expanding efforts to make it harder for identity thieves to get

A man from Canada suffered for years from fraudulent purchases made in his name after the theft of his wallet. Among the purchases were thousands of dollars' worth of KFC fried chicken meals. The thief was finally arrested and charged with multiple counts of identity theft.

the information they want might be a more realistic approach. Many safeguards are available to individuals that will allow them to make their identity more secure. At the same time, the public needs to demand greater accountability from the guardians of its personal data. Acting in concert, government, businesses, and consumers can work to prevent identity theft and make it easier for victims to recover when it does occur.

Facts

- Under the federal Fair Debt Collection Practices Act, collection agencies must stop their activities when notified that a debt is fraudulent.

- The Social Security Administration issues about one thousand new numbers annually as a result of identity theft.

- Unlike credit bureaus, there is no one central clearinghouse for health records. Victims of identity theft must contact each provider individually.

- Many experts also advise filing a report with the FBI, which helps it establish large-scale patterns of identity theft.

- Victims of fraudulent credit card charges have sixty days to appeal the charges.

Source Notes

Introduction: From Riches to Rags

1. Quoted in Jennifer Waters, "Identity Fraud Nightmare: One Man's Story," MarketWatch.com, February 10, 2010. www.marketwatch.com.

2. Quoted in Waters, "Identity Fraud Nightmare."

3. Federal Trade Commission, "Related Identity Theft Definitions, Duration of Active Duty Alerts, and Appropriate Proof of Identity Under the Fair Credit Reporting Act." www.ftc.gov.

Chapter One: What Are the Roots of the Identity Theft Problem?

4. Patrick O'Carroll, "Statement of Patrick O'Carroll, Acting Inspector General, Social Security Administration," testimony before the Subcommittee on Social Security of the House Committee on Ways and Means, June 15, 2004. http://waysandmeans.house.gov.

5. Quoted in Christopher Maag, "The New Breed of Phishing Scams: It's Complicated," Credit.com, February 2012. www.idt911blog.com.

6. Bob Violino, "How to Stop Your Executives from Being Harpooned," InfoWorld, May 23, 2011. www.infoworld.com.

7. Quoted in scambusters.org, "Whaling? These Scammers Target Big Phish." www.scambusters.org.

8. Quoted in John Markoff, "Larger Prey Are Targets of Phishing," New York Times, April 16, 2008. www.nytimes.com.

9. Dawn Hicks, "Vishing: Another Internet Fraud Scam," Federal Reserve Bank of Boston. www.bos.frb.org.

10. Quoted in Fred Mamoun, "Facebook Identity Theft Scam," NBC4Los Angeles, July 7, 2010. www.nbclosangeles.com.

11. Quoted in Mamoun, "Facebook Identity Theft Scam."

12. Quoted in Mamoun, "Facebook Identity Theft Scam."

13. Quoted in Violino, "How to Stop Your Executives from Being Harpooned."

14. Thomas Claburn, "Social Security Number Prediction Makes Identity Theft Easy," *InformationWeek*, July 7, 2009. www.informationweek.com.

15. Quoted in Matt Cullina, "Bin Laden's Death Sparks Cyberscams," *Identity Theft 911 Blog*, May 5, 2011. www.idt911blog.com.

16. Quoted in FBI National Press Office, "Malicious Software Features Usama bin Laden Links to Ensnare Unsuspecting Computer Users," March 3, 2011. www.fbi.gov.

Chapter Two: How Big a Problem Is Identity Theft?

17. Mitch Lipka, "Rise in Identity Theft Tied to Smartphone Use," Reuters, February 22, 2012. www.reuters.com.

18. Ed Dadisho, "Identity Theft and the Police Response: The Problem," *Police Chief*, January 2005. www.policechiefmagazine.org.

19. Ola Olatilu, "Identity Theft and Corporations' Due Diligence," *ISACA Journal*, vol. 6, 2006. www.isaca.org.

20. Frank Abagnale, *Stealing Your Life: The Ultimate Identity Theft Prevention Plan*. New York: Broadway Books, 2007, p. 5.

21. Quoted in Gerry Smith, "Child Identity Theft Takes Advantage of Kids' Unused Social Security Numbers," *Huffington Post*, August 22, 2011. www.huffingtonpost.com.

22. Quoted in Jennifer Sullivan, "Scammers Are Stealing from Elderly by Posing as Grandkids in Trouble," *Seattle Times*, April 18, 2012. http://seattletimes.nwsource.com.

23. Quoted in Jennifer Sullivan, "Scammers Are Stealing from Elderly."

24. James Munton and Jelita McLeod, *The Con: How Scams Work, Why You're Vulnerable, and How to Protect Yourself*. Lanham, MD: Rowman & Littlefield, 2011, p. 161.

25. Laura Bruce, "Identity Theft—Don't Be a Victim," Bankrate.com, October 12, 2005. www.bankrate.com.

26. Quoted in Bruce, "Identity Theft."

27. Quoted in Bob Sullivan, "The Darkest Side of ID Theft," MSNBC, March 9, 2003. www.msnbc.msn.com.

28. Quoted in Bob Sullivan, "The Darkest Side of ID Theft."

29. Mari Frank, *The Complete Idiot's Guide to Recovering from Identity Theft*. New York: Alpha, 2010, p. 7.

30. PatientSecure, "Medical Identity Theft—Stories of Victims." www.patientsecure.com.

31. Michelle Andrews, "Thief vs. Patient," *U.S. News and World Report*, March 17, 2008. www.worldwidebenefitservices.com.

32. Pamela Lewis Dolan, "Medical Identity Theft a Growing Problem," *American Medical News*, October 17, 2011. www.ama-assn.org.

33. Dolan, "Medical Identity Theft a Growing Problem."

34. Jessica M. Pasko, "Years After Identity Theft, Victim Struggles to Clear Name," idchannel.com, January 18, 2012. www.theidchannel.com.

35. Dadisho, "Identity Theft and the Police Response."

36. Quoted in Judy Monchak, "Researcher Finds the Psychological Effects of Identity Theft Lingers with Victims," MedicalXpress.com, April 20, 2011. http://medicalxpress.com.

Chapter Three: How Serious a Threat Are Hackers?

37. Quoted in Terry Frieden, "U.S.: Identity Theft Grows as Hackers Get Savvier," CNN, March 31, 2009. http://articles.cnn.com.

38. GAO, *Report to Congressional Requesters: Personal Information*, June 2007, p. 10. www.gao.gov.

39. Quoted in ITAC, "6 Worst Data Breaches of 2011," blog, December 27, 2011. http://itacidentityblog.com.

40. Quoted in Jessica Silver-Greenberg and Nelson Schwartz, "Visa and MasterCard Investigate Data Breach," *New York Times*, March 30, 2012. www.nytimes.com.

41. Quoted in Bob Sullivan, "EXCLUSIVE: Hackers Turn Credit Report Websites Against Consumers," msnbc.com, March 26, 2012. http://redtape.msnbc.msn.com.

42. Brian Grow, "Hacker Hunters," *Businessweek*, May 30, 2005. www.businessweek.com.

43. PrivacyMatters.com, "Computer Hacking and Identity Theft." www.privacymatters.com.

44. Quoted in Fox News, "Stratfor Hacking Victims Targeted Again After Speaking Out," December 27, 2011. www.foxnews.com.

45. Quoted in Identity Theft Prevention and Education Institute, "Police Web Sites Attacked—a Warning to Us All!," October 22, 2011. http://stolendata.blogspot.com.

46. Martha C. White, "Hackers Now Aiming for Your Credit Reports," *Time*, April 4, 2012. http://moneyland.time.com.

47. Quoted in Jennifer Waters, "What Your Facebook Profile May Be Telling ID Thieves," MarketWatch, January 10, 2011. www.arnoldmachinery.com.

48. White, "Hackers Now Aiming for Your Credit Reports."

49. Quoted in Thomas Claburn, "Hacker Indicted for Stealing More than 130 Million Credit Cards," *InformationWeek*, August 17, 2009. www.informationweek.com.

50. Quoted in James Verini, "The Great Cyberheist," *New York Times*, November 10, 2010. www.nytimes.com.

51. Quoted in Verini, "The Great Cyberheist."

52. Verini, "The Great Cyberheist."

53. Quoted in Verini, "The Great Cyberheist."

54. Quoted in Verini, "The Great Cyberheist."

55. Jared Newman, "Playstation Network Breach: It's Really, Really Bad." Technologizer, April 26, 2011. http://technologizer.com.

56. Quoted in ITAC, "6 Worst Data Breaches of 2011."

Chapter Four: Can Identity Theft Be Prevented?

57. Jo Alison Taylor, "Identity Theft," Legal Counsel for the Elderly, University of Alabama Law School, 2001, 2004. www.law.ua.edu.

58. Quoted in David McGuire, "Bush Signs Identity Theft Bill," *Washington Post*, July 15, 2004. www.washingtonpost.com.

59. US Department of Justice, Office of the Inspector General, "The Department of Justice's Efforts to Combat Identity Theft," Audit Report 10-21, March 2010. www.justice.gov.

60. Office of Representative Jim Langevin, "House Passes Langevin Legislation to Address Foster Youth ID Theft," press release, September 21, 2011. http://langevin.house.gov.

61. Quoted in Electronic Privacy Information Center, "Social Security Protection Act of 2010 Becomes Law." http://epic.org.

62. Social Security Online, "Frequently Asked Questions: Social Security Number Randomization." www.ssa.gov.

63. Quoted in Reuters, "Identity Theft Resource Center Applauds the DoD Military ID Change," April 23, 2008. www.reuters.com.

64. Quoted in Martha C. White, "How Banks Are Aiding and Abetting Identity Theft," *Time*, July 8, 2011. http://moneyland.time.com.

65. Abagnale, *Stealing Your Life*, p. 105.

66. Munton and McLeod, *The Con*, p. 174

67. Stacy Cowley, "If You're Using 'Password1,' Change It. Now." CNNMoney, March 1, 2012. http://finance.yahoo.com.

68. Abagnale, *Stealing Your Life*, p. 123.

69. Ondrej Krehel, "And the Facebook Woes Go On . . ." *Identity Theft 911 Blog*, January 5, 2011. www.idt911blog.com.

Chapter Five: What Are the Challenges of Reclaiming a Stolen Identity?

70. Mari Frank, *From Victim to Victor: A Step-by-Step Guide for Ending the Nightmare of Identity Theft*. Laguna Niguel, CA: Porpoise, 2005, p. 2.

71. Munton and McLeod, *The Con*, p. 179.

72. Frank, *From Victim to Victor*, p. 7.

73. Neal O'Farrell, "12 Reasons Why We're Losing the Battle Against Identity Theft," Identity Theft Council, 2012. www.identitytheft-council.org.

74. Quoted in Emily Jackson, "Man Charged in Identity Theft Spanning Two Decades," *Toronto Star*, September 21, 2011. www.thestar.com.

75. Quoted in US Social Security Administration, "Identity Theft and Your Social Security Number," August 2009. www.ssa.gov.

76. Frank, *From Victim to Victor*, p. 3

77. Quoted in ProtectMyID.com, "Identity Recovery: New Social Security Number," Experian. www.protectmyid.com.

78. Quoted in ProtectMyID.com, "Identity Recovery: New Social Security Number."

79. Quoted in Tracy Kitten, "ID Theft Recovery: Banks Play Key Role," bankinfosecurity.com, November 10, 2010. www.bankinfosecurity.com.

80. Frank, *From Victim to Victor*, p. 60.

Related Organizations and Websites

Anti-Phishing Working Group

PMB 246, 405 Waltham St.
Lexington, MA 02421
e-mail: info@apwg.org
website: www.antiphishing.org

This nonprofit global association combats phishing. The site includes the latest news, consumer advice, and updated warnings about recent scams.

Federal Trade Commission Identity Theft Clearinghouse

600 Pennsylvania Ave. NW
Washington, DC 20580
phone: (877) 438-4338
spam and phishing e-mail: spam@uce.gov
website: www.ftc.gov

The identity theft site of the Federal Trade Commission focuses on deterrence, detection, and defensive measures. The site includes videos and downloadable publications.

The Identity Theft Council

1990 N. California Blvd., 8th Floor
Walnut Creek, CA 94596
phone: (925) 930-3978
fax: (866) 809-4295
website: www.identitytheftcouncil.org

This organization is dedicated to forming a national network of local partnerships among law enforcement, businesses, and volunteers to provide local support to victims of identity theft.

Identity Theft Prevention and Survival

Mari J. Frank
28202 Cabot Rd., #300
Laguna Niguel, CA 92677
phone: (800) 725-0807; (949) 364-1511
fax: (949) 363-7561
e-mail: contact@identitytheft.org
website: www.identitytheft.org

This organization offers advice to consumers as well as information about laws, prevention measures, and more.

Identity Theft Resource Center

PO Box 26833
San Diego, CA 92196
phone: (858) 693-7935; (888) 400-5530
e-mail: itrc@idtheftcenter.org
website: www.idtheftcenter.org

This nonprofit organization provides help for identity theft victims. The website has news stories, general information, and a section called Teen Space, with information geared specifically toward young people.

Microsoft

One Microsoft Way
Redmond, WA 98052
website: www.microsoft.com

Microsoft's official online safety and privacy site offers security updates, free software for spyware removal and other safeguards, tips on safely navigating social networking sites, and more.

National Association of Attorneys General

Consumer Protection
2020 M St. NW, 8th Floor
Washington, DC 20036
phone: (202) 326-6000
fax: (202) 331-1427
website: www.naag.org

The National Association of Attorneys General provides specific information for each state and territory about existing laws, as well as how to file a complaint.

National Council of State Legislatures

444 North Capitol St. NW, Suite 515
Washington, DC 20001
phone: (202) 624-5400
fax: (202) 737-1069
website: www.ncsl.org

The National Council of State Legislatures website shows state-by-state laws and penalties for identity theft.

Privacy Rights Clearinghouse

3108 Fifth Ave., Suite A
San Diego, CA 92103
phone: (619) 298-3396
fax: (619) 298-5681
website: www.privacyrights.org

The Privacy Rights Clearinghouse provides ways of preserving personal privacy and learning about individual privacy rights. Its section on identity theft offers detailed information on prevention and restoration.

US Department of Justice—Identity Theft Information

950 Pennsylvania Ave. NW
Washington, DC 20530
phone: (202) 514-2000; (202) 353-1555
e-mail: askdoj@usdoj.gov
website: www.usdoj.gov

The US Justice Department has the latest information about identity theft and provies numerous other resources, including a simple quiz to test identity theft IQ.

Additional Reading

Books

Frank Abagnale, *Stealing Your Life: The Ultimate Identity Theft Prevention Plan*. New York: Broadway Books, 2008.

Michael J. Arata Jr., *Identity Theft for Dummies*. Hoboken, NJ: For Dummies, 2010.

Ted Claypoole and Theresa Payton, *Protecting Your Internet Identity: Are You Naked Online?* Lanham, MD: Rowman and Littlefield, 2012.

Lamar Coleman, *Identity Theft—Protect Yourself and Your Future*. Seattle: Amazon Digital Services, 2012.

Mari J. Frank, *The Complete Idiot's Guide to Recovering from Identity Theft*. New York: Alpha, 2010.

Bruce Hanson, *Identity Theft*. Seattle: Amazon Digital Services, 2012.

Denis G. Kelly, *The Official Identity Theft Prevention Handbook: Everyone's Identity Has Already Been Stolen—Learn What You Can Do About It*. New York: Sterling & Ross, 2011.

Megan McMally, *Identity Theft in Today's World*. Santa Barbara, CA: Praeger, 2011.

James Munton and Jelita McLeod. *The Con: How Scams Work, Why You're Vulnerable, and How to Protect Yourself*. Lanham, MD: Rowman and Littlefield, 2011.

Bruce Owdley, *Identity Theft Prevention*. Seattle: Amazon Digital Services, 2012.

Jim Stickley, *The Truth About Identity Theft*. Upper Saddle River, NJ: Pearson Education, 2009.

John Vacca and Mary E. Vacca, *Identity Theft*. New York: Chelsea House, 2012.

Internet Sources

Jan Legnitto, "How Online Identity Fraud Destroyed One Man's Life," PrivateWiFi.com, November 15, 2010. www.privatewifi .com/how-identity-fraud-destroyed-one-man%E2%80%99s -life.

McAfee, "What You Need to Know to Avoid Identity Theft." http://au.mcafee.com/en-au/local/docs/AU_ID_Theft_E_ Guide.pdf.

Vanessa Richardson, "4 keys to credit, debit card zero liability policies," creditcards.com. http://www.creditcards.com/credit -card-news/4-keys-zero-liability-policies-debit-credit-1282.php.

James Verini, "The Great Cyberheist," *New York Times*, November 10, 2010. www.nytimes.com/2010/11/14/magazine/14 Hacker-t.html?pagewanted=all.

Jennifer Waters, "Identity Fraud Nightmare: One Man's Story," MarketWatch.com, February 10, 2010. www.marketwatch .com/story/the-rise-of-identity-theft-one-mans-nightmare -2010-02-10.

Index

as federal employee identifier, 24

new, number issued annually as result of identity theft, 78

replacing, problems with, 73–7

social networking sites and theft of, 21

using care in disclosing, 62

Social Security Protection Act (2010), 55–59

Solomon, Diane, 19–20

Sony's Playstation Network, 51

spam filters, bypassing, 14

spearphishing, 14–16

Taylor, Jo Alison, 53

Thornton, Dana, 59

Time (magazine), 9

Tsujihara, Alice, 19

Twitter, 52

unemployed people, scams targeting, 30–31

U.S. News & World Report, 36

Van Vliet, Jessica, 38

Verini, James, 50

vishing, 18–19

Voice over Internet Protocol (VoIP), 18

Wallace, Anne, 34

whaling, 16–18

White, Martha C., 46, 48

Whyman, Scott, 26

Wilkinson, Tom, 76

youth, percentage of identity theft complaints coming from, 39

Picture Credits

AP Images: 28, 55, 70

Bettmann/Corbis: 12

© Owen Franken/Corbis: 19

© Pascal Deloche/Godong/Corbis: 77

© Viviane Moos/Corbis: 21

Thinkstock.com: 7, 32, 44,

© Petros Giannakouris/Corbis: 49

© Andrew Lichtenstein/Corbis: 57

© John Marshall Mantel/ZUMA Press/Corbis: 64

Jim Whiting has published more than 150 nonfiction books for young readers. He has also edited nearly two hundred titles among many genres. His diverse career includes seventeen years publishing *Northwest Runner* magazine, advising a national award-winning high school newspaper, hundreds of venue and event descriptions and photography for America Online, serving as sports editor for the *Bainbridge Island Review*, and writing hundreds of articles for newspapers and magazines throughout the country.